Be Fruitful
AND *Multiply*

Embracing God's Heart
for Church Multiplication

ROBERT E. LOGAN

ChurchSmart
R E S O U R C E S

St. Charles, IL 60174
1-800-253-4276

Published by ChurchSmart Resources

We are an evangelical Christian publisher committed to producing excellent products at affordable prices to help church leaders accomplish effective ministry in the areas of church planting, church growth, church renewal and leadership development.

For a free catalog of our resources call 1-800-253-4276.

CoachNet® is a registered service mark of Robert E. Logan.
All rights reserved.

www.CoachNet.org

Cover design by: Julie Becker
© Copyright 2006

ISBN#: 1-889638-54-4

Be Fruitful
AND *Multiply*

Embracing God's Heart
for Church Multiplication

Contents

Foreword

What About Bob?

When I started knocking on doors that first day I did not have much to say. I just knew people needed Jesus and started banging on their doors to tell them so… and then to invite them to the church we were starting. It was 1988 in the inner city of Buffalo and I did not know what I was doing… and there were few people out there to help.

Years later, I remember hearing Bob Logan tell the story of church planters swimming and drowning and his vision to help them. I remember about six of the guys who started the church planting "swim" with us in those years back in Buffalo and several of them didn't make it. They tried hard, but they just did not know what we know now. When Bob talked about his vision, I wanted to know more… and I am still learning from him.

When I wrote my Ph.D. dissertation on church planting in North America, I noticed that few people talked about church planting systems before the 1980s. Come to think of it, few people talked about church planting before then. Now it is commonplace—dozens of books are available. Back then, there was little out there and Bob Logan changed much of that. As I traced the development of church planting systems in my own denomination, Bob Logan gets mentioned 76 times. The same would be repeated in the study of most evangelical denominations and mission agencies.

What About Bob?

When I think of Bob Logan I think of three things: *pioneering, influencing*, and *waiting*. First, in North American church planting, few of us can mention the name Bob Logan without thinking of *pioneering*. Bob began a new church. Then, he pioneered much of the training that most evangelical groups use for church planting. Then, he pioneered the systems that used training. Now, Bob has a new passion—pioneering a church planting movement. And, if he does it with the same tenacity of his other pioneering ventures, it will be an exciting ride.

Second, Bob has been *influencing*. As a matter of fact, I think Bob is the most influential thinker for North American mission in the last several decades. At first, I thought it was just my tribe/denomination, but as I spoke and consulted with other groups, I saw that Bob was like "Kilroy." Everywhere I went, Bob was there first, leaving his mark like a "Kilroy was here" sketch on the side of church planting systems throughout North America.

Third, I have been *waiting* far too long for Bob to publish his fine work on church multiplication. I have heard him speak, used his resources, and read his articles all the while (impatiently) waiting to get my hands on something that brings it all together in one place. Finally the pioneer has stopped making me wait—and for that I am deeply grateful (and slightly irritated that he did it AFTER I finished the second edition of my own church planting book—citing his OLD system).

Baby Steps

There is little that is done in North American church planting leadership that was not developed or influenced by Bob Logan. Few realize that before his keen insights and organizational acumen, church planters did not go through assessment, boot camps, and coaching networks. Why did Bob do these things? **Because he cares about church planting and church planters**.

In *Be Fruitful and Multiply* Bob reminds us that the gospel is not intended to be a light under a bushel. Instead, it is to be a series of lights spreading and multiplying into communities of darkness throughout the world. If the church would follow his passion (or should I say the passion of the scripture that he promotes) it would be harder to go to hell from North America.

Church planting is not what it once was—the place where you go when you can't find a real church job. But, it is not what it should be—the normal practice of New Testament churches. For thirty years we have taken baby steps toward true biblical church planting but books like these will help us break through to movements.

I'm Sailing!

I like to read books about carpentry from carpenters, sports by sportsman, and practice from practitioners. Simply put, there is no one in North America who has lived church planting like Bob Logan. When he speaks, I listen and when he writes, I treasure—and so should you if you value reaching North America.

Honestly, Bob and I are not friends. I have spent ten minutes with him in person… but many, many hours learning from him. His ministry has created the tracks that my ministry train follows and for that I consider him a friend. Thanks, Bob, for yet another gift to the church in *Be Fruitful and Multiply*.

Like the Bill Murray character in the movie "What About Bob?," Bob Logan taught us all how to take "baby steps." Now, *Be Fruitful and Multiply* teaches us how to move from churches starting churches to true church planting movements. That's a quantum leap forward—but a needed one if we are to truly see the gospel transform North America. As in the movie, it's time to move from "baby steps" to "sailing," and I for one am ready. Thanks, Bob, for your ministry and for this new gift to the church.

Ed Stetzer is the Missiologist and Director of the Center for Missional Research at the North American Mission Board. His most recent books are *Planting Missional Churches* **and** *Breaking the Missional Code* **(with David Putman).**

Acknowledgements

Many thanks to all the church planters and denominational leaders who were willing to be interviewed during the research stage of this book: Steve Pike, Don Davis, Ed DeLong, Gary Craig, Dave Holland, Lee Brockington, Glenn Bleakney, Mike Perkinson, Sean Adams, Don Allsman, and Marc Shaw.

Thanks also to the many others I've worked with over the years...as your stories have interfaced with my own, they have become part of the fabric of my ministry experience. Steve Ogne served with me in the early years of developing church planting systems. Tom Johnston provided leadership in helping me organize the years of experience into a unified and more comprehensive set of resources found in the "Cultivating Church Multiplication Movements" network within CoachNet (*www.coachnet.org*).

Colin Noyes, my CoachNet partner in the South Pacific, provided valuable insights and persistent encouragement throughout the entire project. His energy and enthusiasm for the project served as a strategic catalyst for us.

Special recognition and appreciation goes to Tara Miller, who conducted numerous interviews and served as the primary writer for this book. Evan Drake helped me put the finishing touches on the manuscript.

Julie Becker did her usual excellent work on the cover design and layout.

I am grateful for the ongoing partnership with Dave Wetzler and ChurchSmart Resources. His friendship and belief in me serves as a constant source of encouragement.

And how do I say thanks to my wife, Janet? Words cannot express my gratitude for her influence on my life.

It is my prayer that this book will stimulate people to take the next steps toward starting and multiplying healthy churches among all peoples...to God be the glory!

Introduction

In the movie "Pay It Forward," a young boy is assigned a class project to improve mankind. He decides that if he can do three good deeds for someone and they in turn can "pay it forward" and so forth, positive changes can occur. His action sparks a multiplying movement of change.

Likewise, in *Disciples Are Made, Not Born*, Walter Henrichsen describes a display at the Museum of Science and Industry in Chicago. This display features a checkerboard with one grain of wheat on the first square, two on the second, four on the third, then eight, 16, 32, 64, 128, and so on. Somewhere down the board, there was so much wheat that it was spilling over into neighboring squares so the display ended there. Above the demonstration was a question: At this rate of doubling each square, how much grain would you have on the checkerboard by the time you reached the 64th square? To find the answer to this riddle, you punched a button on the console in front of you, and the answer flashed on a screen above the board: Enough to cover the entire subcontinent of India, 50 feet deep!

Church multiplication is part of the very fabric of what it means to be a church. God has always intended for His living creation to be fruitful and multiply, and filling the earth and the church is certainly no exception. But what is church multiplication?

In this book I'd like to stretch your thinking to embrace the possibility of much more fruitfulness for God's kingdom than you ever could have imagined.

Because I care deeply about the expansion of God's kingdom through the church, I have devoted much of my life's work to aiding the multiplication of churches in one form or another. I've been a church planter, I've coached church planters, I've developed resources for church planters... yet more and more I've come to see that the calling of God on the church goes beyond church planting. Church planting isn't enough. If one church is planted and then the process is over, that won't be enough to fulfill the great commission. Jesus called us to go and make disciples of all the nations. That means not just a few more churches, but many more... exponentially more. I've become increasingly convinced of God's call on the church to engage in church multiplication—those great movements of God where churches plant churches that plant more churches that plant more churches.

My purpose in writing this book then is two-fold. First, I hope to convince the unconvinced. Many Christians have never heard of church multiplication or, if they have, they have not given it much thought as something God is calling them to be a part of. I believe that the call of God on every Christian's life is to be part of a church multiplication movement, regardless of what form that involvement may take. In the first half of this book, I lay out the basic concept of church multiplication and discuss its biblical roots. While exploring the various ways church multiplication can look in different contexts, I also highlight the underlying principles that transcend context. Finally, I discuss the many different ways God has called us to be involved in church multiplication; we all have a different role to play depending on our spiritual gifts, personality, interests, and calling.

Secondly, in the latter half of the book, I take those who are interested in launching a church multiplication movement one step deeper. Although this section does not include everything that is needed to orchestrate a multiplication movement, it provides a basic framework for getting started. The second half of this book walks readers through the ten essential areas of a church multiplication movement, including action steps and recommendations for further resourcing.

So who should read this book? Anyone who is interested in finding out more about God's larger calling for the church—cultivating church multiplication movements. The book is particularly helpful for denominational leaders, apostolic pastors, and lay leaders who want to discover their role in this great work of God. So read part 1 prayerfully, then if you are convinced that a multiplying church is God's plan—not just another human endeavor—go on to part 2 and discover how you can begin making changes in the right direction.

PART ONE

Why multiplication?

————

Chapter One

Seeing the possibilities: movements of God within the church

The Methodist movement

Imagine within your lifetime a move of God where thousands and thousands of people come to know Christ. The harvest overflows. New small groups and churches begin forming, but so many people are becoming Christians so quickly that there aren't enough existing leaders to meet all their needs. New leaders are raised up from the ranks of the new believers and they take on responsibility for overseeing the new churches.

That's what happened through the ministry of John Wesley, a traveling evangelist in England in the 1700's. So many thousands came to know Christ through his preaching that he had to form new groups and churches—and he had to use new converts to lead them. He developed reproducible approaches that enabled them to function effectively as leaders while they learned. They grew into their leadership as they continued to serve, evangelize, make disciples, and raise up more leaders from the harvest. Out of Wesley's work came a whole movement of churches called the Methodists.

In his lifetime, Wesley saw 72,000 people in England and 57,000 people in the United States become followers of Christ. But this was just the beginning. In the generation after his death, countless thousands more came to know Christ through the churches he left behind. At one point, one in every 30 adults in England was a Methodist. Wesley's movement continues to this day. People are still coming to Christ who can trace their spiritual heritage directly back to the ministry of John Wesley.

New Life Fellowship

Mike Neuman tells this amazing story.

SOURCE: Mike Neuman, *Home Groups for Urban Cultures* (Pasadena, CA: William Carey Library, 1999)

New Life Fellowship (NLF) was a church founded in Bombay by Pastor S. Joseph in 1968. By 1980 the church had only about 100 members. However, they then began emphasizing church multiplication. As of 2000, there were approximately 1,200 house churches in 250 worship centers with an estimated attendance of 50,000. The churches own little property—both the worship centers and the church offices are rented. NLF has become a nationwide church multiplication movement with churches in most major cities, all 26 states, and several countries outside India.

In 1985, Pastor Shanthkumar Williams was sent out to plant another New Life Fellowship in Miraj, India. There he discipled and raised up other church planters, and from that first church plant in Miraj, churches continue to be planted and multiplied. There are now more than 80 NLFs in the region. These churches meet in homes or rented premises and vary in size between 30 and 150 members.

Awakening Chapels

In 1998, Neil Cole, pastor of Awakening Chapel in California, began with the question: "How do we reach people with the good news of Jesus Christ?" Neil and his team began visiting a nearby coffee house several times a week and building relationships. People began to open up to spiritual things, and the group started offering evangelistic Bible studies designed to reach postmodern people. As more and more of these people came to know Christ, Neil and his team gathered them together in what they called an organic church. As this church grew to overflowing, they started more organic churches.

To follow up on these new Christians, the team used a simple process called Life Transformation Groups. Two to four people come together regularly for scripture reading and accountability. No training is needed to lead these groups. Designed to multiply, the groups branched off whenever a fifth person wanted to join. Within five years, life transformation groups were functioning on all seven continents.

Neil and the team help people grow step by step into leadership, raising up leaders from among the converts through a continual discipling, mentoring, and coaching process. These organic churches have continued to multiply and have birthed whole new movements as well. Collectively, these movements now come under Church Multiplication Associates. When I asked Neil how many of these organic churches are still in existence, he said he couldn't give exact numbers because they are multiplying so fast, but he knows of at least 375 spread over twelve countries in less than four years.

Conclusion

Church multiplication movements can happen anywhere, anytime. They adapt to the cultures, they raise leaders from the harvest, and they build multiplication into the genetic code. What made the difference in each one of these movements? Why were they successful? It was Wesley's critics who identified the secret: they were the ones who began calling his followers the Methodists. It was not a compliment, but a derogatory label. Yet they had accurately identified the element that set his ministry apart: a simple, reproducible method—a system that empowered ordinary people to do extraordinary things.

When Jesus commanded his disciples to make disciples in Matthew 28, he was telling them to do what he had done and continue the process. What did Jesus' disciples do in response? "They devoted themselves to the Apostles teaching.... and enjoyed the favor of all the people. And God added to their number daily those who were being saved" (Acts 2:42-47). "So the churches were strengthened in the faith and grew daily in numbers" (Acts 16:5). They multiplied churches. Disciple-making already has multiplication built in on the personal level—the multiplication of groups and churches simply moves it up to the next level.

You can be a part of a great movement of God, cooperating with his Spirit, living out his church the way it was intended to be. The seeds of church multiplication can start with just one person coming to Christ. Consider the story below, adapted from *Leading and Managing your Church* by Robert E. Logan and Carl George.

In 1977 Paul Okken, a pioneer Baptist missionary to Rwanda, returned from Africa for medical aid. During the most recent five years of his ministry, 60 new churches had been started, and the number would climb to 80 by 1980. "How did God direct you to the area for this remarkably fruitful harvest?" he was asked one time. One day before the planting had begun, Okken said, he was driving, overlooking a huge valley inhabited by many tribal people. He was an evangelist by gift and calling and felt a burden for all the people living in clusters across the valley. With a deep sigh, he prayed, "Oh God, what's to become of all these lost people?" Unexpectedly, from the empty passenger seat beside him he heard the answer, "Ask Me for them."

Not being accustomed to hearing such voices, Okken dismissed the matter and continued his drive. He came to another bend in the road over-looking the valley. Once more he was compelled to ask the question, "Lord, what's to become of these people?" Unmistakably a voice replied again, "Ask Me for them."

Paul Okken was a supernaturalist, but not a Pentecostal. True to his Baptist roots, he decided to put this "special revelation" to a reasonable test. "God if this is really from you, I'll go down there and preach—if even one person is converted, I'll feel you are guiding me and I'll spend more time preaching here." Then he prayed, "Oh God, give me the souls of these people for Jesus."

In that very first preaching event, *eleven* adults responded to their first hearing of the gospel. It was the beginning of a great harvest.

Through that one Baptist missionary and his followers, the Holy Spirit started 80 churches. These leaders developed a method from a very simple New Testament theology: the concept of the congregation as a body with discernible parts. Whenever a person came to Christ, the missionary assumed God wanted a body of believers established there. At the first convert, the missionary team did not know if they had uncovered a hand or a leg. So they would continue evangelizing, until they could discern in the new believers' group enough of a body, with its various functional parts, to make a viable church.

At one point, the team of missionaries wanted to move on, but Paul told them, "No, we can't leave here yet. That man is the one who God has given the pastoral gift to care for the flock, and he's not a Christian yet. We have to keep coming back here until he gets saved." It's such a simple concept: every time there is a new convert, you have discovered an elbow, a kneecap, or a nose. The assumption is that the rest of the body must be nearby and a church will emerge through evangelizing the new convert's network of relationships. Through any one person, you can find the seeds of a new church.

Using this approach, the 80 churches existent in 1980 became 160 churches by 1985. That's the beginning of a multiplication movement. With this evidence of movements sprouting around the world, we can look at their roots to understand how they can be replicated.

Chapter Two

Biblical roots

God's idea

Church multiplication is not just some new fangled idea—it's biblical. It was God's idea from the beginning. If church multiplication is just the latest ministry fad, you might as well put this book down right now. But it's much more than that. After extensive study of God's word, I am convinced that church multiplication is an idea deeply rooted in scripture.

Genesis 1 says, "Be fruitful and multiply." From the beginning, God intended for us to multiply. Everything that is living and healthy is designed to multiply: animals, plants, people. Family trees branch out, then that influence spreads all over... you never know where. They continue to grow and spread, just as plant and animal species continue to grow and spread. That's part of God's design.

We see this principle throughout the Bible. God said to Abraham, "I will make you the father of a great nation. Your descendants will be as numerous as the stars in the sky." Abraham passed down an important heritage to his people. Jesus was eventually born from his line. Abraham's influences were felt.

Just as we multiply physically, we also multiply spiritually. Jesus instituted spiritual multiplication when he told us to make disciples. That was Jesus' plan: he spent time with his chosen twelve disciples, then left them with the great commission—essentially a charge to pass along his influence, his spiritual DNA, his family tree. As individual believers, we are called to make disciples and multiply. Our life can be so much more than what we alone can accomplish if we invest in others. And what's true of individual believers is also true of churches: we are called to multiply our groups and ultimately our congregations. That's the story of the book of Acts.

The early church

Let's do a brief overview of the Apostle Paul's missionary journeys and you'll see what I mean. Neil Cole, in a paper titled, "A Fresh Perspective of Paul's Missionary Strategies: The Mentoring for Multiplication Model," examines the ways in which Paul's missionary journeys changed over time. We don't often think of Paul as a learner, but he was. If you look carefully at his missionary journeys, you can see his growth process. You see him learning from mistakes, you see his strategy shifting, you see him making transitions, and you see his vision becoming more and more long-range. With each journey, he focused more of his time and energy on mentoring, coaching, and raising up leadership. Through this process, he becomes increasingly fruitful during the later stages of his ministry.

On the first missionary journey, Paul and Barnabas (and John Mark for a time) worked as traveling evangelists, going from town to town, making converts, and starting churches—the original church-planting missionaries. Church growth was done by addition—convert-by-convert, church-by-church—but that addition was significant. Thousands converted, including future church leaders such as Timothy, Titus, and Luke. The missionary team ran into their share of snags, including John Mark abandoning the effort partway through. And they had little time for follow-up with the churches that they left behind or with potential future leaders. But with such numeric success, who wouldn't repeat such a journey? That appears to have been the plan for Paul and Barnabas: a second missionary journey just like the first one.

But that wasn't what God had in mind. God forced the multiplication of the team: Paul and Barnabas had a sharp disagreement over whether or not to allow John Mark back on the team after he had left the last time. Barnabas took John Mark, Paul took Silas, and they went their separate ways.

In addition to Silas, Paul recruited Timothy and Luke as well. And off they went with the intention of continuing as itinerant evangelists—with Asia high on their list of places to go. But God would not allow Paul to enter Asia yet—he had something to teach him first. God essentially trapped Paul in Corinth, whittled down his team until he was alone, and then made this wandering evangelist stay put for a year and a half.

Left without any other viable options, Paul for the first time raised up a church planting team from the harvest itself. It was there that he met Priscilla and Aquila, shared the gospel with them, mentored them, and sent them out to start new works for the kingdom. Then he watched as Priscilla and Aquila raised up Apollos, who quickly became known as a powerful preacher. Paul took note of the incredible value of raising up other leaders and sending them out. He found his ministry was twice as effective with one other leader, three times as effective with two other leaders, and so on. Suddenly this vast untapped potential was opened up before him. During his time in Corinth, Paul's strategy shifted from making converts to raising up leaders from those converts.

With this valuable lesson in mind, Paul realized that all he needed for his third missionary journey was himself. He went to Ephesus, took up residence, and focused entirely on mentoring and multiplying leaders who could be sent out to reach the harvest. The success of this third missionary journey was unprecedented. From Ephesus, Paul reached all of Asia Minor. As it says in Acts 19, "the whole region of Asia heard the Word."

What was happening in Ephesus? How did one man effectively reach the entire Asia Minor region in just two or three years without having left the city? Essentially, Paul launched a church multiplication movement. Let's look at six of the things he actually did:

1. **Established a regional base of church planter development.** Acts 19:8-10: "Paul entered the synagogue and spoke boldly there for three months, arguing persuasively about the kingdom of God. But some of them became obstinate; they refused to believe and publicly maligned the Way. So Paul left them. He took the disciples with him and had discussions daily in the lecture hall of Tyrannus. This went on for two years, so that all the Jews and Greeks who lived in the province of Asia heard the word of the Lord." After being kicked out of the synagogue, Paul set up his training hub at the School of Tyrannus—likely a school of philosophy owned and run by someone named Tyrannus. Tyrannus allowed Paul to use the school during the hot afternoon hours while others were resting. He taught daily in the school of Tyrannus for two years. Because Ephesus was a strategic urban center, many people from surrounding areas and surrounding cultural and racial groups took up residence in the city. If you could reach Ephesus, you could by extension reach the whole surrounding region.

2. **Developed a teaching/mentoring strategy by life example.** Acts 20:19-20: "I served the Lord with great humility and with tears, although I was severely tested by the plots of the Jews. You know that I have not hesitated to preach anything that would be helpful to you but have taught you publicly and from house to house." Paul's teaching style was up close and personal. People knew him; they

watched him as he wrestled with difficulties and adversity. And Paul taught not only publicly, but also from house to house. This was someone who really let people know him—they could watch to see how he practiced what he preached.

3. **Used evangelism & discipleship to train leaders.** Acts 20:21: "I have declared to both Jews and Greeks that they must turn to God in repentance and have faith in our Lord Jesus." The message was direct and specific and was paramount to the foundation that produced churches through out Asia Minor.

4. **Allowed the Holy Spirit to lead the emerging leaders into ministry.** Acts 20:28: "Keep watch over yourselves and all the flock of which the Holy Spirit has made you overseers. Be shepherds of the church of God, which he bought with his own blood." Paul recognized that it was not him who called people to the ministry, but the Holy Spirit. As he watched these leaders start churches and raise up his spiritual grandchildren, Paul—like a good grandparent—recognized that he was not in control. He released those leaders and their churches to the care of the Holy Spirit.

5. **Mentored individuals on a one-to-one basis.** Acts 20:31: "So be on your guard! Remember that for three years I never stopped warning each of you night and day with tears." People develop at differing rates. Emerging leaders don't all start and finish together at the same time. Paul mentored people individually over time—for years—admonishing and warning them, telling them what they needed to hear in the moment. This kind of tailor-made approach, impossible to duplicate in a classroom, meets leaders where they're at and focuses on what they need to learn at that particular time.

6. **Empowered his leaders with accountability to God.** Acts 20:32: "Now I commit you to God and to the word of his grace, which can build you up and give you an inheritance among all those who are sanctified." Even Paul had to say goodbye. These people he had lived with for years had to go forth and do the work God had for them, and Paul released them to do that. He committed them to God because he knew that God had a call on their lives.

And what an amazing call it was—Ephesus became the mother church to all the churches of Asia Minor. The success of this movement was unprecedented. From Ephesus, Paul trained the future leaders of the church... many of the names we recognize from the New Testament.

Epaphras was trained at the school of Tyrannus, and then he went out to start the church in Colossae. Philemon was also trained at Tyrannus. And there are dozens more names: Trophimus, Tychicus, Archippus, Nympha, and Apphia.... the list goes on. These people went out to start more and more churches throughout Asia Minor until—as it says in Acts 19, "the whole region of Asia heard the Word." There was clearly a saturation of church planting going on—a church multiplication movement. And Paul, still in Ephesus, wrote letters to churches he had never visited, but that were born out of the movement he began: his spiritual grandchildren. The churches that grew out of this movement were not dependent on Paul, but were self-governing, multiplying churches.

Passing it on today

Acts records the beginning of church multiplication. It's in the DNA of the church—part of God's plan from the start. Only through multiplication could Christianity go from being a few hundred outlaw followers of Jesus to being the official state religion of the Roman Empire—its influence felt world-wide—all within its first 300 years.

Church planters and pastors should be told from the beginning that healthy churches reproduce—it's a biblical concept. A general rule of thumb is that new churches should plan to plant another church within the first three years of their life as a church. The likelihood of a new church planting another church diminishes significantly after three years. The church in Antioch had not gotten very large when they were led by the Holy Spirit to send out Barnabas and Saul, their first missionaries and most outstanding leaders, to plant churches. Acts 13:1-3: "In the church at Antioch there were prophets and teachers: Barnabas, Simeon called Niger, Lucius of Cyrene, Manaen (who had been brought up with Herod the tetrarch) and Saul. While they were worshipping the Lord and fasting, the Holy Spirit said, 'Set apart for me Barnabas and Saul for the work to which I have called them.' So after they had fasted and prayed, they placed their hands on them and sent them off."

Engaging in multiplying churches means taking risks—sometimes financial risks, sometimes the risk of giving away people, and always the risk of shifting your focus from your own congregation to the wider work the Lord is doing. That's the primary shift in thinking that is required for churches to be intentionally engaged in multiplication—turning from an inward to an outward focus. Even brand new churches that are small, struggling finan-cially, and not yet ready to multiply can find creative ways to be involved in new church planting efforts.

Just months after launching, one church knew it didn't have the resources to become a parent church yet, but they did commit to sending prayer teams into neighboring communities where the groundwork was being laid for new church plants. Later they volunteered to lead worship for a new plant during its first three months of public services while training some of their lay people who had gifts in that area. By being involved from the very beginning and actively looking for ways to help new church plants in any way they could, the people in that congregation kept their focus outward and their hearts open to the idea of multiplying. They focused their vision on church planting and regularly asked themselves, "What is the best way for us to participate in that vision right now?"

Multiplication is inherent in the creation principle: everything reproduces after its own kind. The true fruit of an apple tree is not just an apple, but another apple tree. A person can count the number of seeds inside one apple, but only God can count the number of apples inside one seed. Just as disciples reproduce disciples and ministries reproduce ministries, churches reproduce churches. It may seem to be a big shift to go from being inwardly focused to being outwardly focused, but it's clearly a biblical one. God will honor a commitment that extends beyond the local church to the universal church.

Chapter Three

What is a multiplication movement?

Hope Chapel

Five years ago, Hope Chapel sent out one quarter of its congregation (350 people) to start two new churches... two weeks before moving into a new building. Since then, they've planted at least one church a year by hiving off 100 to 150 people each time. One of the new churches is running about 600, with the smallest just over 100.

In the meantime, one of Hope Chapel's daughter churches planted four more churches in Japan. Other daughter churches continue to plant, in Hawaii, Japan, the Philippines, and New England. In New England, the lineage goes seven generations deep and they've become a movement of their own with nearly 20 churches planted.

However, the greatest numerical success is in a place where the Holy Spirit had to pull it off or it wouldn't have happened. Paul, a golfing buddy of one of the multiplication movement leaders, went on a business trip to Pakistan and began mentoring a man with the gift of evangelism (and 120 converts to prove it). The man's name was Salamat, and he was discipling his converts by email whenever he could afford to log on at the internet cafe. The Lord told Paul to tell Salamat that "he is not an evangelist, he is an apostle. And that those are not his converts, they are my pastors." Paul gave him the word and Salamat immediately planted a church in Karachi. It now numbers over 500 people and they have planted more than 90 churches since early 2001.

Hope Chapel is now reinvestigating Japan where they have 19 church starts. Their goal is to see 100 in the next twelve years. They also believe the 300+ churches in the entire movement could reach 1,000 by that time.

How did Hope Chapel do this? They look primarily among "minichurch leaders," those who demonstrate fruitfulness in evangelism, discipleship, and multiplying leaders in a small group setting. Then the pastoral team prayerfully considers these people and asks the Lord which of them he is calling to become church planters. The candidates that emerge are engaged in dialogue and asked to pray about God's call for them. Those who express interest are gathered into small groups for specialized development that involves reading books, discussing them together, and life mentoring. The benefit of this approach is that their initial pool consists of people who have proven their character and ministry potential. The small group is the church in microcosm—an ideal environment for finding leaders.

Multiplication vs. addition

Consider the potential inherent in multiplication rather than addition. Do you remember learning the multiplication tables? For months you'd been painstakingly working on addition: $5 + 5 = 10$, $10 + 10 = 20$. Eventually you'd probably hit 30 or so, but how long would it take to get to 100 or 200 or 300? Those numbers seemed rather out of reach. But then came multiplication. Suddenly there was momentum, acceleration. With this method, suddenly those big numbers didn't seem so unattainable anymore.

The same principle holds true for churches. Adding new churches is good—multiplying new churches is better. Multiplying churches means planting churches that go on to plant other churches, that go on to plant other churches, that go on to plant other churches. That's how addition becomes multiplication. When you tally it up, the long term potential is astounding.

Recently a greater emphasis has been placed on church planting, yet most material on church planting is still based on growth by addition. The churches that get planted often do well and reach the lost, but they seldom become church planting churches. Another school of thought emphasizes growing healthy churches that grow. Disciples make other disciples, leaders train other leaders, groups give birth to other groups, and ministries plant the seeds of other ministries. This is the natural order and progression of growth. However, many stop short of recognizing that churches should continue to grow beyond their own walls. They are designed to start other churches. And those churches are designed to start more churches, which will go on to start yet more churches.

Most pastors think about growing healthy churches or growing large churches, but they typically don't think of growing multiplying churches. A significant paradigm shift is required to move from growth by addition to growth by multiplication. For the best way to reach the harvest isn't through large churches, or even through planting more churches, but through churches that multiply—whatever their size.

The kingdom of God, alive in his church, is organic. It's designed to live and grow and reproduce. Disciples, groups, churches… all have a part in fulfilling the great commission. Disciples multiply other disciples, groups multiply other groups, churches multiply other churches… all with one end in mind: to reach the whole harvest for Jesus Christ. To move from growth by addition to growth by multiplication, we must begin looking at our churches from a kingdom perspective.

Church multiplication movements like Hope Chapel start with a change in thinking. Most people I talk to believe the hope of Christianity lies in strong local churches. That's true but it's only part of the process. Where do local churches come from? Jesus has called us to carry the message of the gospel to every nation and every people group. We often apply this command to missions, but not to the local church—forgetting that they are one and the same. Local churches need to see that their role in fulfilling the great commission is to grow beyond themselves to create more local churches.

But what about church health?

The most common questions raised about church multiplication involve concern about the health of existing churches. "We aren't healthy enough ourselves to be involved in church planting." "We've got enough work to do in our own church." "We don't even have the leaders we need to fill volunteer positions here." "We need to deal with our internal problems first." "We can't even meet our own budget needs." These are important, legitimate questions that most people wonder about.

Thankfully, God has not left us with an either/or choice: either we focus on health or we focus on multiplication. God has designed the process so they both go together and mutually enhance one another. Healthy churches multiply and multiplying churches become healthier. Not only is multiplication biblical, not only is it more effective than addition, but it also increases the health and growth of local churches that participate.

In fact, multiplication is a necessary, essential step toward healthy maturity. Consider Japan, in which less than 1% of the population are believers, sending planters to Indonesia, which is comprised of 18% believers. Does that make any sense? It does—for the church in Japan is richer and more vital for the sending. "Church planting acts as a sign and bringer of maturity. A church is not mature until it is involved in taking the gospel out beyond its own cultural or geographical boundaries," according to church historian Dr. Paul Pierson.

NCD (Natural Church Development) research has conclusively found that multiplying churches are healthier than non-multiplying churches. The health scores on the NCD survey for churches that multiply are consistently higher than the scores for those that haven't. Cell-based churches, which are founded on a principle of multiplication and tend to plant more churches, were also found to be healthier. A recent survey by NCD found that multiplying churches also continue to grow at a faster pace than non-multiplying churches, even when they give away people. A recent study found that, within a five-year period, for every 25 attendees, multiplying churches gained 9 new attendees while non-multiplying churches gained only 5. That's a growth rate that's almost twice as fast, even without accounting for the people given away to start new churches.

Source: The Institute for Natural Church Development International at www.ncd-international.org.

A denominational leader puts it this way: "Church planting is fulfilling in the same way that having a child is fulfilling to parents. Churches see themselves fulfilling their God-given role. When a church knows its reason for existence and fulfills that destiny and purpose, it's incredibly encouraging." Concerns about church health no longer need to be a deterrent for beginning to plan for church multiplication.

An established suburban church helped plant a church in a lower income, ethnic, urban area. The newly planted church quickly developed an exceptionally high quality worship team. That team has cross-pollinated neighboring churches and is now training outside worship leaders, spurring growth and positive change throughout the denomination. That new church plant has given people a vision for how church multiplication can revitalize existing churches.

Let me underscore again that church health is a legitimate and important concern. We all want healthy churches. And in some cases, churches can become extremely unhealthy. Often the dissatisfaction created by poor health can be a needed impetus for moving forward. People in unhealthy churches need the renewed hope of a better future that church multiplication can provide.

A church founded in the 1920s sits in the inner city of Hollywood. At its zenith, it was the church of Hollywood stars like Roy Rogers and Dale Evans. Over the years, the neighborhood changed and the church started declining. Eventually, attendance dropped down to just 25 people, the church was $280,000 in debt and had a negative cash flow of $3,000 per month, and they were about to close their doors. The congregation knew they had to change or die. As a last ditch effort to save the church, they called a new pastor, a man who has seen radical transformation in his own life. They were so desperate they agreed to follow his leadership completely.

When the pastor preached his first sermon, he came walking in with a sledgehammer and started talking about the problem with idols. "In the Old Testament, when people needed to repent of worshipping idols and change their ways, they were told to destroy those idols. I've prayed long and hard over this issue, and I've come to the conclusion that one of the idols here is the choir." Then he took the sledgehammer and began pounding holes in the nice solid wood of the choir loft. After about ten minutes of swinging the heavy hammer and working up a good sweat, he turned to the people and asked, "Well? Are you going to help me clean up this mess?" It took five years for the church to become debt free and operate with a positive cash flow. They give over 20% of their income to local and global missions.

Today, ten years later, the church is thriving with over 200 people. They've planted another church that runs about a hundred adults. They share their facilities with other congregations who are also involved in birthing new churches. The people at this inner city church are poor, but no other organization in Hollywood except the Salvation Army feeds more people every week. Twice a day they host a meal and offer everything they have to whoever will come. They have a vision to establish a church plant- ing training center with an urban focus. They want to raise up leaders who will know how to minister incarnationally in environments of incredible diver- sity. Within a twenty-minute drive of that church, you can almost reach the entire world.

This Hollywood church is a church multiplication success story—yet it all began with a dissatisfaction with church health. God calls us to look beyond difficult present circumstances and to embrace the vision for a better future. He has called all churches to both health and multiplication. Far from being mutually exclusive, the two qualities go hand in hand. Healthy churches multiply and multiplying churches become healthier.

Three key ingredients of church multiplication movements

1. **Multiplication movements are empowered by God.** Supernatural involvement is necessary. Whenever you see a multiplication move- ment, God has to show up. Jesus said, "I will build my church," and "Apart from me you can do nothing." We see throughout the book of Acts how God's people look to him in prayer, and then see his supernatural power unleashed. Our work alone is not even close to sufficient. Only God can change a life, much less a group or a church or a movement of churches. Reliance on his empowerment is essential.

2. **Multiplication movements are culturally relevant.** They must connect to the hearts of people. For lives to be changed, the needs of the people must be addressed and met. What is the good news for this particular group of people in this particular place and time? I remember training a group of church planters for multiplication movements. I said to them, "I am a member of your target group, I'm not a Christian, and I have one question for you: What's the good news?" If they started talking about theological issues that didn't relate to where I was in the first twenty seconds, I'd interrupt and say, "You just lost me." I had already concluded that their message is irrelevant—that they have nothing for me.

I still remember one man's response; a planter bound for Salt Lake City, Utah, the center of Mormonism. That's among the tougher places to start a church in the U.S. I asked him, "What's the good news for the people in Salt Lake City?" He looked me right in the eye and said, "Bob, through Jesus Christ you can realize your full potential and you don't have to fit into anybody else's mold." That sent shivers up and down my spine because in Salt Lake City, Utah that's not just good news, that's great news! That you could experience freedom in Christ, you could have the release of sin, you could see all that God has made you to be and express that fully and uniquely. That's the kind of transforming power of the gospel that people can't help but spread to those around them. That's what I mean by cultural relevance. If our message cannot be contextualized, it will not be heard. The Apostle Paul writes about the importance of adapting our methodology to our culture:

> *[19]Though I am free and belong to no man, I make myself a slave to everyone, to win as many as possible. [20]To the Jews I became like a Jew, to win the Jews. To those under the law I became like one under the law (though I myself am not under the law), so as to win those under the law. [21]To those not having the law I became like one not having the law (though I am not free from God's law but am under Christ's law), so as to win those not having the law. [22]To the weak I became weak, to win the weak. I have become all things to all men so that by all possible means I might save some. [23]I do all this for the sake of the gospel, that I may share in its blessings.*

3. **Multiplication movements use reproducible methods.** As described at the beginning of this chapter, reproducibility is the cornerstone of any successful church multiplication movement. Whether it's disciples, leaders, groups, ministries, or churches, all must multiply. Reproducibility empowers ordinary people to do extraordinary things. As harvest comes in, capacity increases. With that capacity, more ministry is done, and more of the harvest comes in. Reproducibility is the principle behind it all. I saw an ad one time with a picture of a golden egg and above it the caption read, "What you really need is the goose." A great ministry is wonderful. But what you really need is the principle of reproducibility that creates more and more great ministries.

Chapter Four

Leaders: the essential foundation of a multiplication movement

The need for leaders

In Honduras, new believers are baptized right away in obedience to the biblical pattern described in Acts 2:37-41: "Repent and be baptized.... Those who accepted his message were baptized, and about 3,000 were added to their number that day." While still dripping wet, new converts newly baptized are told, "You died with Christ, and now the power of the resur-rected Jesus is in you. That power can help you overcome the sinful patterns in your life. What sinful habits do you have in your life that you need the power of Jesus to help you with?" In this way, new believers are taught to begin listening to the Spirit right away, becoming sanctified so their lives continue to change to reflect the power and presence of God. They are then told, "Since you are witnesses to the power of Jesus, who do you know who needs what you have? What are you going to do about that?" And so they are thrust into ministry right away. New Christians are eminently qualified to be a witness. They need no training, for a witness just testifies to what they've experienced. New converts keep working on their personal issues and they keep working in ministry. Simple and reproducible: making converts, making disciples, making leaders.

The number one limiting factor in reaching the harvest is leadership. The future of the church is in its leaders. Any church multiplication move-ment that wants to multiply churches must also find a way to multiply leaders, for it will quickly run out of existing, ready-to-go leaders. Creating solid, reproducible methods for raising up indigenous leaders from the harvest will feed and sustain a church multiplication movement.

In Matthew 9, Jesus says, "The harvest is plentiful but the workers are few. Ask the Lord of the harvest, therefore, to send out workers into his harvest field." A lack of workers is the major blockage Jesus identifies. And how do we overcome that blockage? How do we get workers? By asking God for them. James tells us that sometimes we have not because we ask not (James 4:2). Since praying for workers is one of those prayers that we know for certain is God's will, we can pray with faith and confidence that he will answer us. Whenever believers start seriously praying this prayer, God begins raising up people to be involved in church multiplication in one form or another.

If it is God's will that we ask him for workers, and if he will answer us when we pray in his will, the key question becomes: how much are we really asking? The fundamental reason we often don't ask is found within the context: we ask not for the workers because we care not for the harvest. Jesus saw the people, felt compassion, and asked the Lord for workers. There's a direct linkage between the compassion we feel in our hearts and our motivation to plead with God for the necessary workers.

Then, flowing from that compassion and those prayers, is the action necessary to raise those workers up. It's no accident that the very next passage, Matt. 10, shows Jesus taking action to raise up leaders and send them out into the harvest fields. The apostles, remembering Jesus' example, later did the same. Who founded the church in Antioch? In Alexandria? In Rome? No one knows. The apostles didn't plant those churches them-selves. They were established by now-anonymous lay people. The word had gone on ahead of the apostles, carried by ordinary people whose lives had been touched by the power of the gospel.

Deliberate leadership multiplication

How do you raise up leaders while doing evangelism and making disciples? How can they be simultaneous, yet deliberate? Remember the story of the Awakening Chapel house church multiplication movement from the first chapter? Neil Cole raised up leaders from among the converts he was reaching, and they have begun multiplying churches themselves. We can see the results: hundreds of churches in just a few years. But how did that happen? What is the engine that drives that kind of growth? The integra-tion of evangelism and leadership development.

The core team of the original church focused first on evangelism. They did numerous things to further that goal: taking prayer walks, hanging out where unbelievers are, building authentic relationships with people, sharing the gospel, starting evangelistic Bible studies using the book of John. When people come to Christ, they are baptized right away. The leadership then gets new converts involved in life transformation groups (LTGs) of two to four people. These groups involve reading scripture, confessing sin, and praying for others. As people's lives continue to change and the LTGs multiply, those who are on a demonstrated path of spiritual development and who are fruitful in seeing new groups get started are recognized as potential leaders. Those potential leaders are deliberately coached to accelerate their development. The coaches look at both ministry and personal development, and ask, "What are the next steps for you in loving and obeying Jesus?" As they work with leaders, they have in mind a checklist for a fully developed leader. Only when the leaders they are coaching begin coaching others do they receive that checklist.

The organizing principle of multiplication is raising leaders. Neil Cole's tag line is, "First things first, one thing at a time, always one more thing." By following people systematically, step-by-step through the process and starting with the end in mind, leaders are raised up. The process of leadership development is woven seamlessly into evangelism and discipleship. Over time, fruitful well-rounded leaders are formed.

*Note: More information on this method of leadership development can be found in "Raising Leaders for the Harvest," by Robert E. Logan and Neil Cole (St. Charles, IL, ChurchSmart Resources, 1996)

Indigenous leaders

Raising leaders for the harvest cannot be overemphasized. Raising leaders from the harvest also cannot be overemphasized—strong, indigenous leadership, leadership that is of the people, is what cements a church and keeps it going during times of difficulty. The absence of that kind of leadership creates a vacuum, leaving a church vulnerable to the attack of outside forces.

The church in North Africa during the first few centuries was comprised of three layers of people, each representing a different segment of the population. First were the Romans and those who had assimilated completely into Roman culture. We know many of the Roman leaders of the North African church quite well: St. Augustine, Cyprian, Tertullian. Next were the Carthegenians, descendants of Phonecian sailors. They were from Carthage, which was destroyed by the Romans. The Carthegenians made up a smaller percentage of the church and some church leaders came from that group. Finally, before the Romans, before the Carthegenians, were the Berbers. They were the indigenous desert people of North Africa. By Roman definitions, the Berbers were the lowest level of civilization. There were few Berber Christians, and almost no Berber leadership in the church.

How could Islam have swept so quickly through North Africa and obliterated that strong North African church that gave us leaders like Augustine? The reason may be that it was a relatively elitist church penetrating somewhat into the conquered Carthegenian population, but not much at all into the original indigenous population.

When we think about mobilizing leaders for a church multiplication movement, we need to recognize two realities. First, the leaders need to come from the harvest. We will quickly run out of pre-trained, ready-to-go leaders once multiplication really takes off. Second, these leaders need to come from the ministry focus groups we are trying to reach. Nothing will handicap a movement and prevent ownership faster than leadership imported from the outside.

The missionary histories of Korea and China exemplify this principle. In China, missionaries came in on the waves of western imperialism. Missionaries could enter China only because of the unequal treaties forced upon China by England and other western powers. Consequently, missionaries in China were often identified with western imperialism.

Korea was different. Missionaries started arriving in Korea in 1884, just at the time Japan was beginning to attempt to dominate Korea. By 1910 Japan had annexed Korea, and Korean Christians took the lead in the movement toward independence. There was no conflict between being a Korean nationalist and being a Korean Christian—there was, in fact, an alliance. Due to strong Korean leadership that had been raised up from the harvest, Christianity was not seen as an external force, but as a movement arising from within the culture. Leadership matters. And mobilizing that leadership well can make or break a church multiplication movement.

In the 5th century, Ireland was considered the domain of barbarians. These people could never become true Christians, believed the Romans. They were uncivilized, illiterate, politically unorganized. They couldn't be Christianized, and they certainly couldn't become Christian leaders. They were unreachable.

Patrick, an English priest who had previously been a slave in Ireland, thought differently. He used his understanding of the Celtic people to indigenize the faith, using the language, customs and stories of the people both to reach them and to help them give expression to a growing faith. He and a small band of other Christians settled in or near a village, ministered in ways that would appeal to the Celtic culture, stayed for a few months, baptized believers, built a church, and raised up an indigenous leader to pastor the church. When Patrick and his band moved on to the next village or tribe, they often took a few young people from the community along as apprentices.

In this way, Patrick and his band launched a church multiplication movement. His 28 years of ministry in Ireland saw roughly 700 churches planted and 1000 Celtic priests ordained. The fact that Patrick understood the people and their culture and raised up indigenous, multiplying leadership most likely accounts for the strength and expansion of Celtic Christianity.

*Source: *The Celtic Way of Evangelism: How Christianity Can Reach the West... Again* by George G. Hunter III (statistics from p. 23)

The Roman church wanted to civilize people and make them fit certain cultural norms before they experienced Christianity. Patrick did the opposite. He brought the Celts to Christ, helped them grow through their own culture and released them to minister to their own people. Many churches today want people to fit cultural norms before they get involved in ministry. We have to do the opposite. We have to empower indigenous leadership— people who are not like us—and release them. That may feel like a big risk, but it's the only way to get a true multiplication movement off the ground.

Leadership development

This shift in thinking has implications for leadership development as well. To a large extent, raising leaders for many churches begins and ends with finding sufficient people to fill the missing holes in the church programs. Multiplication helps us shift our focus from inward to outward: we're not raising leaders for our church, we're raising them for the churches of the future—those that have yet to be established. And many of these new leaders will have to come from the ranks of the new believers who are then introduced to simple, reproducible methods that empower them to multiply disciples, groups, ministries, and churches.

Carol Davis is a woman who has been connected to church multiplication since her childhood. A few years ago, she met Charles Brock, a successful multiplication movement leader in the Philippines. "I have a question I've been wanting to ask you for four years," she said. "You plant churches rapidly, they produce leadership from within, they are not dependent on outside funding, and they reproduce. I know others plant churches in these same areas. It takes years, the churches stay dependent on outside resourcing, they import their leadership, they say, because poverty has destroyed the psyche of the people and they are not leadership quality. These churches do not reproduce. I want to know why you can do it and they can't"

The answer, which Davis expands upon in her article "Starting Church-Starting Churches," lies in raising up indigenous leaders from the harvest and releasing them to reach others and begin ministering right from the beginning. In John 1:43-45, we read that Jesus found Philip and told him, "Follow me." Philip's first act was going out to find Nathaniel and tell him about Jesus. If we wait too long to empower others for ministry, they are often reluctant to try. Releasing people from the harvest to reach others and begin to minister right away is often what makes the difference between church planting and church multiplication. Charles Brock said, "I never do anything that a one-week old Christian can't do. If I preached like I did in my home church they would think they couldn't carry the gospel until they had my skills, my training."

Church multiplication movements—those that reproduce quickly and spread among the people—can be best led by grassroots movements of ordinary believers doing what Jesus called them to do. Leaders are the future of a church multiplication movement. If the leadership is strong, the movement will be strong. Mobilizing leaders from the harvest who have a vision and a zeal for the harvest is one of the best assurances of the continued progress of a church multiplication movement.

Chapter Five

What's my role?

Where do I fit in?

Possibly you are reading this book and recognizing the need for church multiplication, but thinking, "But God hasn't called me to be a church planter or a leader of church planters. Where do I fit in?" Good news—God has given every believer an integral role to play in church multiplication, whether or not they are a planter or leader of planters. It is with good reason that the apostle Paul writes in I Corinthians 12:

> [14]Now the body is not made up of one part but of many. [15]If the foot should say, "Because I am not a hand, I do not belong to the body," it would not for that reason cease to be part of the body. [16]And if the ear should say, "Because I am not an eye, I do not belong to the body," it would not for that reason cease to be part of the body. [17]If the whole body were an eye, where would the sense of hearing be? If the whole body were an ear, where would the sense of smell be? [18]But in fact God has arranged the parts in the body, every one of them, just as he wanted them to be. [19]If they were all one part, where would the body be? [20]As it is, there are many parts, but one body.
>
> [21]The eye cannot say to the hand, "I don't need you!" And the head cannot say to the feet, "I don't need you!" [22]On the contrary, those parts of the body that seem to be weaker are indispensable, [23]and the parts that we think are less honorable we treat with special honor. And the parts that are unpresentable are treated with special modesty, [24]while our presentable parts need no special treatment. But God has combined the members of the body and has given greater honor to the parts that lacked it, [25]so that there should be no division in the body, but that its parts should have equal concern for each other. [26]If one part suffers, every part suffers with it; if one part is honored, every part rejoices with it.

[27]Now you are the body of Christ, and each one of you is a part of it.

Since God has created the church to function as a body, every part of that body must play its part if the whole is to be healthy and reproduce. An intercessor is no less important than a planter; one with the gift of giving is no less important than one with the gift of leading. All believers must come together and contribute their gifts, for all gifts and all believers are essential for the call of God to a church multiplication movement to be realized. Although a full treatment of all gifts and roles is beyond the scope of this book, some of the more common ways believers can support a church multiplication movement are discussed in this chapter. As you will see, multiplication movements embrace a broad range of gifts and people.

Praying for the harvest and the church

Why have so many church planting movements floundered with lack of finances, poor results and burned out planters (or even worse) when Jesus said, "I will build my church and the gates of hell will not prevail against it"? Somehow we have not prevailed as we should have. Perhaps spiritual dynamics are the key. We need Spirit-filled planters entering communities prepared by prayer and engaging in work supported by heartfelt intercession.

Most of the church has plugged into the relational side of prayer, enjoying communication with their heavenly Father. To foster a multiplication movement and bring in the harvest, we must tune in more intentionally to the working side of prayer. There are those in the body of Christ for whom intercession is the good work that God has prepared in advance for them to do. (Eph. 2:10). Help is urgently needed for intercessors to do their work.

Prayer is not an add-on, but an essential. It forms the foundation and the bedrock of any multiplication movement. Without prayer, human plans will come to nothing. Throughout history, every successful church multiplication movement has been conceived and nurtured in prayer. The Moravian Movement, under the leadership of Count Zinzindorf, began as a prayer meeting in 1727. Known as the Hourly Intercession, it involved relays of men and women coming before the throne of God 24 hours a day. That prayer meeting lasted for 100 years. It also resulted in action, especially evangelism. More than 100 missionaries left that village in the next 25 years, all constantly supported in prayer.... Within 20 years, the Moravians had sent out more missionaries than all the other Protestant groups combined in the last 200 years.

More recently, the DAWN movement was begun in the Philippines in 1974. At that time, they set a goal of multiplying the current 5,000 churches in the country to 50,000 by the year 2000. During the 1990s, the goal of 50,000 churches was surpassed. What happened that produced such an increase in church multiplication?

In 1980 God inspired a group of intercessors from three churches in metro Manila to spearhead strategic intercession for the nation. From this small beginning a national prayer movement was born called "Intercessors for the Philippines," led by Bishop Daniel Balais. Its mission is to equip, mobilize, and network the Body of Christ in the Philippines to intercede for the nation to fulfill its destiny as truly a Christian nation and a launching pad of missionaries to Asia. The group organizes interdenominational prayer meetings, holds annual national prayer gatherings, offers hundreds of prayer training seminars, and provides detailed prayer guides with specific prayer items from movement leaders. The result was 50,000 churches. Prayer made all the difference.

Multiplying churches—churches that storm the gates of hell and set captives free—is a spiritual battle fought on a spiritual plane. The stakes are high, the enemy is determined, and we are not strong enough to overcome him alone. God must be with us if we are to succeed. Through prayer and the renewing of our minds, we can tap into the power of the Holy Spirit to change hearts and break down strongholds. Prayer is the essential foundation upon which multiplication movements are launched.

A church planter tells the following story, "When I raised support, I also raised prayer. In just about every church I visited, I found an intercessor who really latched onto my ministry. I'd communicate once every two months through a newsletter, and at least once a week I'd get cards in the mail—usually from some little old lady—saying, 'God put you on my heart today and I'm praying for you.' And I am absolutely confident that without that prayer, there is no way we could have seen the successes we've seen. We're planting in an extremely resistant area where it usually takes decades to reach the 200 or 300 point in a new church. If we'd had 50 people after a year, I'd have considered it an extraordinary success. After our first year, we had 80. After four years we had 200. After ten years we had 600. And we've been involved from the very beginning in planting new congregations as we've grown. There is no way that could have happened without prayer. Prayer cannot be an afterthought—it needs to be part of the infrastructure."

Positive, practical actions on the part of leaders, supported by intercessors, are a key to spiritual warfare within a multiplication Movement. Spiritual strongholds can be expressed in the mindsets and attitudes of people as well as in more widespread oppression in the community. Prayer and worship will break down these barriers. "For our struggle is not against flesh and blood, but against the rulers, against the authorities, against the powers of this dark world and the spiritual forces of evil in heavenly realms" (Ephesians 6:12).

Spiritual revival only and always starts with prayer. Church multiplication movements push back the kingdom of darkness and expand the kingdom of light until we see victory expressed in people coming to Jesus and a transformed community. That mission requires prayer, for any advance of the kingdom brings opposition in many forms.

Many external factors will impact leaders. An ever deepening prayer life for leaders in your churches will empower them to negotiate the coming challenges. Possible opposition may include personal temptations, family struggles, sin in the congregation, false accusations, resistance to giving (money, people, time) to church multiplication efforts, and time-consuming crisis in the lives of individuals or the life of the congregation. While these problems are a part of any ministry, intercessors and leaders need to recognize when they indicate direct opposition and have a spiritual life cultivated to confront and overcome that opposition.

As believers begin to deepen their prayer life, they will need to look inward as well as outward. Just as there are blockages to cultivating a spiritual atmosphere that nurtures a church multiplication movement, so there are barriers that need to be negotiated as people deepen their prayer life. Certain ways of thinking can set themselves against our ability to know God intimately (2 Corinthians 10:3-5). As all who are involved in church multiplication deal with personal mindsets and struggles in their relationship with God, they will begin to operate out of a greater peace and security in God.

As anyone in ministry can attest, some things happen only because of prayer:

"I was a 26 year old seminary student leading a Bible study. I discipled three other men as they took on leadership responsibilities, and the Bible study mushroomed into two different groups with 50 people in each. The people began to pray hard that I would turn the Bible study into a church plant. I didn't want to do it because I thought I was too young. I wasn't even finished with seminary—who was going to listen? I fought it all the way, but the Lord released it and I finally got on board.

"We started as an independent church plant with 100 people, an average age of 27, and a grand total of $600. We tried to rent a facility—a 7th Day Adventist Church—for $1500 per month. They turned us down. After a few weeks, we went back and said, "We've prayed and we really believe God wants us to be in this place." The pastor went back to the board and they decided to give us the space on a trial basis. However, the conditions had changed. The rent was now $200 per month for the first three months, Sundays only. After that, if the arrangement worked out, they'd give us an office and access six days a week for $750 a month.

"We began holding services and took in over $4000 our first month. People were getting saved. It was a lot of fun—a bunch of young people who had no idea what we were doing. Eventually we bought the building. All of that because people were faithful and prayed. I call it the accidental church plant, because I didn't really want to do it. The plant took off on us and it really messed up my last year of seminary."

With this beginning, the planter went on to multiply more churches out of the one he started and is now actively involved in coaching planters for church multiplication movements. Some things happen only because of prayer—it is the root and lifeline of any work of God. As the Apostle Paul wrote, "Finally, brothers, pray for us that the message of the Lord may spread rapidly and be honored, just as it was with you." (2 Thessalonians 3:1) Paul understood that human effort alone could not get the job done. Ultimately, church multiplication movements are a spiritual process, not a human one.

Cultivating hearts

A denomination set big goals for church multiplication and revitalization. They cast a lofty, far-reaching vision and talked a great deal about the need for more new churches. But when it came time for acting on those goals, they were reticent to free up money or release people. The leaders said it was important, but wouldn't make the tough calls necessary to move forward. Their talk was a lot bigger than their walk.

Most groups only have compliance to a vision, not true commitment to it. Developing and focusing that shared vision is essential to the success of a multiplication movement. Without actively cultivating a vision for church multiplication, a would-be movement never gets off the ground. It will remain a nice idea that we may do someday when we have the time.

Many among the body of Christ are called to participate in casting vision for church multiplication and cultivating hearts. Generally speaking, two things prevent shared vision for church multiplication: one is not seeing the harvest (vision) and the other is not caring for the harvest (heart). Seeing the harvest means seeing it in its entirety—in all the diversity that exists—and noticing where God's hand may be at work. Caring for the harvest means having a compassion for the lost that reflects the heart of God.

Vision and heart: the two are inextricably linked—one cannot flourish without the other. People must see the harvest in order to care about it, and they must care about it in order to really see it. It's a symbiotic relationship. Sometimes the problem is more one of blindness—people don't see the whole harvest. Sometimes the problem is more one of the heart—they see but don't care. Yet the two are always linked. Vision casters will need to do enough cultivating of the heart for people to be able to see the harvest, and enough looking at the harvest to develop true compassion.

The best way to begin is with the heart. Out of a true heart for the harvest will grow a desire to identify the harvest more specifically, which in turn will lead to a deeper compassion. Synergy develops as each side strengthens the other, and leaders will constantly need to be moving back and forth between heart and vision. Then, when both heart and vision are in place, leaders will need to cultivate a faith that the harvest can be won—the faith that is needed to take action.

I once sat down with a few leaders to take a look at a major urban center and was reminded of how people can look at the same city and see completely different harvest fields. No one sees the whole thing, but everyone sees important facets. One leader looked at the city culturally, seeing all the different ethnic groups. Another viewed it economically, taking note of where the rich are and where the poor are. A third leader took a generational approach, focusing on where the different populations are moving as they reach different stages of life. No one person sees the whole mosaic—and that's okay. It's going to take all kinds of churches to reach all kinds of people. But if a person or group has a heart for the harvest, they will see the harvest and respond with action.

Whatever specific strategies are used to create a shared vision for church multiplication, people must be encouraged to see the harvest and to care for the harvest. One without the other will not be enough. To move forward in the vision, we must see the people God wants us to reach and have a compassion for the lost that reflects the heart of God.

When these two elements are fused to create a strong vision for church multiplication, the foundation for a movement is created. The Foursquare denomination in Nigeria is strong and growing. As a direct response to a conference on church multiplication, the Nigerian church leadership sent a missionary to the United States to begin multiplying churches in urban areas where Nigerian emigrants are moving. They recognized a need for more churches and said, "You know what? We can help." They are about to launch a third Nigerian church plant in Chicago: a four-month-old church is birthing another church. That's the beginning of a movement.

Broadening horizons

Sometimes God places people in our midst who push us to broaden our horizons. They act as prophets, calling us to see what we do not want to see. Casting vision and cultivating hearts for church multiplication is the first important step, but then we need to take a closer look at the harvest. Who exactly is God calling us to reach? In some cases, the answer may make us uncomfortable. Sometimes God calls us to cross-cultural church multiplication.

Current effectiveness or receptivity may give us clues as to appropriate ministry focus groups, but that should not be a limiting factor if God is stretching our boundaries. A predominantly black church in a suburban area felt God's call to plant a church in a racially diverse urban neighborhood. It was just as hard for that church to plant in an unfamiliar culture as it is for any white congregation. The church faced significant challenges, both external and internal, but God blessed their efforts. Regardless of color or class, cross-cultural church multiplication is difficult, yet sometimes that's what God is calling us to do.

We need to be careful not to overlook sections of the harvest. Consider all of the harvest and be open to hearing God's call to reach out to different ministry focus groups. That may mean committing to address spiritual blockages within congregations. Ethnocentrism—the viewing of one's own culture as central and primary—is usually unconscious, and it's hard for people to become aware of their own cultural biases. The Apostle Peter didn't recognize his without the help of God and others. Certain people groups or geographical areas that have been either consciously or unconsciously avoided may need to be reconsidered. In some cases when a particular target group has been unfairly overlooked, self-evaluation and repentance are an appropriate starting point.

A regional director for a denomination was interviewing church planter candidates in an attempt to broaden the geographic scope of church multiplication in his region. He asked planter after planter, "How would you feel about planting in the Deep South, maybe rural Mississippi or Arkansas?" After the tenth candidate declined, he shook his head and said jokingly, "Seems like God's not calling anybody to plant in the rural south. I guess he just doesn't want to do any work there."

Likewise, some mainstream middle class churches have genuine doubts about the legitimacy of reaching out to urban areas. They harbor the often unconscious belief that urban culture itself is corrupt. Yet cultural differences are just that—differences. It's not a matter of better or worse, godly or ungodly. God calls his church to reach all areas and all people groups—

not just those we are initially comfortable with. In some cases, we will be most effective reaching those who are like us. In other cases, God has called us to step out in faith and plant churches cross culturally in order to reach a broader spectrum of people. Much listening prayer will be required to discern his voice.

A wealthy, established church near a large metropolitan area considered their planting options and chose a difficult, but ultimately rewarding, ministry focus group. They planted a church in a poor, unreached urban community. The differences in terms of economic, social, and educational backgrounds were significant, and all pre-evangelism was done by congregants of the mother church. Why did they make the choice they did? In reading the scriptures, they realized there were more verses on the poor and the Christian's responsibility to them than there were on angels or heaven or even prayer, and they felt God's call to reach the poor right next door. They had been supporting the poor overseas, but realized they were much more creative about overseas missions than they were about cross-cultural church planting in their own immediate area.

In most cases, proximity can be an advantage. Having nearby churches in the same denomination can be a big support in terms of prayer, encouragement, and ministry. There's not a suburban church near a major city anywhere that's not within a 45-minute drive of a community that has little or no evangelical presence.

In cases where church multiplication crosses cultural barriers, an awareness of certain biblical principles is essential. When Paul and Barnabas returned from their first missionary journey in Acts 15, they were thrilled that Gentiles were accepting the message of the gospel. Yet some Jews objected, saying, "If Gentiles accept the gospel, they must also accept Jewish culture and law. They must be circumcised." A sharp debate ensued: this was the first critical theological and missiological issue in the early church. The Spirit spoke, and made it clear that the Gentiles did not need to become Jewish in order to become Christians. They did not need to change their culture.

Yet one of the most common errors throughout church history has been to force people to change their cultures in order to become Christian. The Romans tried to Romanize before Christianizing. The English criticized Hudson Taylor, missionary to China, for dressing in Chinese garb instead of trying to "civilize" the Chinese. Some western missionaries attempt to bring capitalism overseas along with Christianity. Christians reared within traditional churches often insist that new converts sanctify their musical tastes, exchanging contemporary music for hymns.

Instead of trying to change people's cultures to make them fit in better with established churches, we need to establish more churches that are culturally relevant: we need a church for every culture. The idea is a biblical one. Jesus came to a specific group of people—politically oppressed Jews of the 1st century—and tailored his message in such a way that they could hear it. He then commanded us to carry that message to every nation. Indeed, God makes it clear in the book of Revelation that he will purchase people from every tribe and language and people and nation (Rev. 5:9). We need to present the gospel in such a way that unbelievers can hear it from within their own cultures. Then they will be empowered to create churches consonant with their culture—churches that feel like home.

Jesus said, "Do you not say 'Four months more, and then the harvest?' I tell you, open your eyes and look at the fields! They are ripe for harvest." (John 4:35) We need to recognize the diversity of those harvest fields—culturally, linguistically, economically, generationally. It will take a lot of different kinds of churches to reach everybody. One church or denomination won't be able to reach everyone alone. That's why multiplication is needed. By developing vision for different segments of the harvest, we can start targeting specific groups that need to hear the good news—the good news for them.

If you are one of those people who God has given a heart for cross-cultural ministry, consider casting a vision among your congregation. Often God places you strategically where he has work to do and calls you to raise up others to share in that work.

Multiplying groups

The small group forms the relational cornerstone of the church community—this is where much of the evangelism, discipleship, and leadership development of the church takes place. Small group leaders have an integral role to play in a church multiplication movement.

If you are a small group leader, consider your group a microcosm of the church. You can make more and better disciples, you can raise up leaders, one of the people you influence for Christ might become a church planter, or you might discover you're a planter. It's possible you could help form the seeds of a new church. As you multiply groups and leaders, be sensitive and open to what God might be doing in and through you.

As shepherds of one of the smallest multiplying units of the church, small group leaders can also cast vision through modeling. People may fear church multiplication less if they see the successful multiplication of a small group. Often group members can even take justifiable pride in their group's multiplication: "Our group was so great it got too big and we had to make two groups out of it! Wow—we really have something to offer!" The small group is the core of the church; what takes place there begins taking place church wide.

Developing planters

In the last chapter we talked about the importance of raising leaders. After all, a successful church multiplication movement will require many, many leaders. As we look for ways to generate those leaders, consider that leadership development is everyone's business. Developing, assessing, and coaching leaders for church multiplication is a team effort involving many different skill sets and gifts.

Developing

Developing leaders begins with evangelism. It continues with discipling new Christians. It includes having someone lead a Bible study. Training isn't just one intensive event—it's really more about the whole process of developing church planters from the very beginning. You're training planters when you teach people how to evangelize and how to multiply small groups. Think of the whole process of training as a giant iceberg. The final formal training class is just the tip of the iceberg— the most visible part. The real work of developing those leaders is 90% below the surface. And the exciting thing is that you don't know at the beginning who will be church planters—so treat everyone as if they might be one.

Assessing

The number one reason why churches fail is getting the wrong planter. Planter selection is crucial. The consequences of poor selection are profound, not only in terms of dollars invested, but also in terms of damage to people's lives—the planter, their family, and the core team. The effects of a failed planting effort create a ripple effect, affecting everyone involved. Assessing church planters well is critical to the process. And often someone with skills sets different than a planter will be the one with the eyes to discern.

> If anyone sets his heart on being an overseer, he desires a noble task. Now the overseer must be above reproach, the husband of but one wife, temperate, self-controlled, respectable, hospitable, able to teach, not given to drunkenness, not violent but gentle, not quarrelsome, not a lover of money. He must manage his own

family well and see that his children obey him with proper respect.
—1 Timothy 3:1-4

Most of us have read this passage many times. And yet what does it mean? Is this checklist of character qualities and teaching gifts all there is to assessing a leader? Many Christians are people of strong character, yet are not called to be overseers, planters, or pastors. In assessing potential leaders, we must take into account the whole context of scripture. Different gifts lead to different functions within the body: "Just as each of us has one body with many members, and these members do not all have the same function," Romans 12:4

Church planters do need to have strong character. But they also need certain skills and competencies, a calling from the Lord, compatibility with the sending organization, placement in the right context, and relationship with the right coach. Leaders can also look quite different from one another, and different from what one would expect. Paul had a history of persecuting Christians. John Mark failed and yet was called back into ministry.

Assessing leaders is a complicated business, to say the least. Much wisdom is called for. Jesus took time to pray before choosing his disciples. Because it is so important to lay hands on the right people, the Lord needs to provide discernment about who to choose and not choose.

Coaching

Just as some are gifted assessors or interviewers, others are gifted coaches.

Without someone helping us stay on track, we can lose sight of our vision in a very short time. We forget why we're doing what we're doing. We get discouraged and want to give up. It's so easy to lose our perspective and become sidetracked from our chosen path. That's true for all of us, and church planters are no exception. In fact, given the magnitude of the task they are undertaking and the resistance they are likely to encounter from the enemy, planters are especially vulnerable to becoming sidetracked from their vision. Regular, intentional coaching is the piece of the puzzle that helps planters get on track and stay on track.

"The purposes of a man's heart are deep waters, but a man of understanding draws them out," writes Solomon in Proverbs 20:5. That's the role of a coach: to be that person of understanding who draws out the purposes of another's heart. Coaching is the process of coming alongside someone to help them discover God's agenda for their life and ministry, and then cooperating with the Holy Spirit to see that agenda become a reality. Coaches focus their energy on helping others succeed. For a biblical model, look to Barnabas. By encouraging and challenging others, he empowered them for ministry. Barnabas may not have been in the starring role, but without him many others would not have been able to accomplish the great things for God that they did.

Coaches come alongside people to help them reflect on their goals and refocus their activities toward that end. Coaching is not about telling people what to do, but about giving the gift of listening and then asking good questions that help people listen to God for themselves and find their own solutions. We all need those types of relationships in our lives, but they are essential for planters. This type of encouraging, empowering relationship is what allows planters not to just keep their heads above water, but to thrive and ultimately to multiply themselves. Coaching makes a huge difference for planters—both qualitatively and experientially.

Planters show improvement with coaching. A recent denominational research study by Ed Stetzer demonstrated that planter coaching resulted in a broader ministry impact in terms of church growth (measured by attendance). New church developers who met weekly with a mentor or coach started churches that were almost twice the size of those who did not meet with a mentor.

Even without research data, planters understand the impact of coaching on an experiential level. I was talking with a church planter and asked him what the most helpful thing a parent church or a denomination did for him during the planting process. He didn't even have to stop and think. He replied, "Coaching. Coaching was the single most helpful and beneficial resource I had. Money was nice, but meeting with my coach once a month was by far the most important."

So what qualities are important in potential coaches? Good coaches are people who can be trusted, people who are perceived as caring. Look for those who naturally empower others and are helpful to them, those who can listen well and ask good questions, and those who don't feel they have to tell others what to do. Ask yourself if this is a person who can resist the temptation to tell his or her own stories. For the issue isn't how the coach did it—the issue is what God is calling this new planter to do.

Consider the checklist below from Steve Ogne and Tom Nebel in *Empowering Leaders Through Coaching*.

Look for people who:
- Have good character
- Share vision and values
- Are loyal
- Are respected by other leaders
- Empower others for ministry
- Have a teachable spirit
- Have the ability to lead a ministry
- Have the ability to multiply ministry
- Have the ability to listen and care
- Have the ability to strategize and train
- Have the ability to challenge and confront

Avoid people who:
- Have a problem with pride
- Need to lead rather than coach
- Need to control others
- Are over-committed to other ministries

Giving of ourselves and our resources

Fundraising is a word most pastors dread. Money isn't everything in church planting, but some of it is certainly necessary. Yet giving extends far beyond money. Just as church members give not only of their finances but of their time, talents, and other resources as well, so people can give in those same ways to church multiplication. A human resources specialist may donate her time in conducting assessment interview; a small group leader may contribute to church multiplication by discipling new believers; a pastor may release leaders from their own congregation to form the core team of a new one. The ways of giving are as varied as the body of Christ itself. We bring our spiritual gifts, our natural talents, our position in life, our relational network, our background and training.... everything we are we can bring to the table. Just as we have freely received, so we are to freely give.

Countless biblical passages extoll the benefits of giving for the giver.

> *"One man gives freely, yet gains even more; another withholds unduly, but comes to poverty. A generous man will prosper; he who refreshes others will himself be refreshed."* (Proverbs 11:24-25)

> *And again from the New Testament: "Yet it was good of you to share in my troubles. Moreover, as you Philippians know, in the early days of your acquaintance with the gospel, when I set out from Macedonia, not one church shared with me in the matter of giving and receiving, except you only; for even when I was in Thessalonica, you sent me aid again and again when I was in need. Not that I am looking for a gift, but I am looking for what may be credited to your account. I have received full payment and even more; I am amply supplied, now that I have received from Epaphroditus the gifts you sent. They are a fragrant offering, an acceptable sacrifice, pleasing to God. And my God will meet all your needs according to his glorious riches in Christ Jesus. To our God and Father be glory forever and ever. Amen."* (Philippians 4:14-20)

The giving of money specifically is often a touchy subject among planters and lay people alike. Yet some believers are called to give generously in this way. Remember that people who give are not doing planters a favor or supporting a pet project. They are participating in God's plan for his church, and will be blessed through their giving. The practice of generosity is an opportunity for growth and obedience in the lives of all believers. That shift in thinking makes it much easier to actively pursue funding for church planting, whichever side of the equation you are on.

Just as many individual believers are called to give financially to church multiplication, so are newly planted churches. Yet that can be extremely challenging. Much faith is required to be generous when you don't know how your own operating expenses are going to be covered. One young church found itself in the position of sending out their key associate pastor with 50 people and their tithes, plus another

$100,000 at the same time that they were buying a new building for themselves.

The senior pastor remembers sitting down at a board meeting and going over the numbers. "We still had the mortgage on the old building, we were losing 50 people and their tithes, and we were increasing our monthly need with the new building. The bottom line was a $6,000 per month increase in expenditure without any visible means to pay for it, and we were giving away that much in tithes and offerings. It didn't make sense on paper—it looked like suicide on paper. I remember looking up at the members of the board after running the numbers and asking, 'Does this make sense?' Their basic response was, 'No, it doesn't make sense. But we feel called to do it and we believe God's going to help us.'

"That was a huge step for our church in terms of our commitment to multiplication. And I still don't know how this happened, but over the next few months, our income actually went up even though we lost all those people. We never missed a beat. We just kept on going and the church continued to grow. It was phenomenal to see how God took care of us. On top of that, the church we planted, planted another church almost immediately in the same community. The commitment to multiplication had become part of the genetic code and was passed down to the next generation."

God sometimes calls us to dramatic steps of faith in giving to church multiplication, whether that involves giving of our money, our time, our talents, our resources, or our leaders.

Chapter Six

Moving forward

Church multiplication around the globe

Church multiplication is not just for the exceptional church, the mega-church, the specially gifted church, but for ALL churches. It's God's call on all the ordinary churches all over the globe. Churches everywhere are bound by Jesus' call to take the gospel across the street, across the city, across the ocean. Wherever you see evangelism, growth, and vibrancy, you see the multiplication of new churches.

Australia

Over a period of ten years, an average suburban church with a seating capacity of 200 planted three churches. The first one was the hardest because it involved giving away 35 people. The new church grew and the mother church was back to 200 people in four months. The second time seemed easier because the church now had a success-ful planting experience that demonstrated how God could be faithful. The pattern repeated itself: they gave away 40 people and within three months attendance was back to 200. With the third plant, the church was ready for a greater step of faith: they gave away one of the pastoral staff and 70 people. It took seven months this time, but the church again grew back to the 200. All three church plants are strong and healthy, with two of them larger than the mother church and one now at 600 in attendance. The last church is in the process of planting another church.

Honduras

Amor Viviente—"Living Love"—is a church in Honduras that has established 18 congregations during the past 18 years—one a year. Yet these congregations are also starting new congregations. They've multiplied overseas, starting churches in Costa Rica, New York, New Orleans, and Miami. One of the congregations is building an auditorium to seat 6,000, yet Carlos Marin, church president, emphasizes the church's priority will remain on growth groups—that's the smallest multiplying unit and the root of all the rest of the growth.

> Reference: **Pulse, January 8, 1993.** *"Honduran church growing through house fellowships"* **by Nathan Hege.**

Armenia

In the early 20th century a series of traumatic events in Armenia damaged the region's churches. Armenian national genocide along with Soviet communism tried to destroy anything religious. Christian leaders were harshly persecuted and church buildings destroyed. Nevertheless the church was not extinguished. In fact, recent history has seen an unprecedented growth of churches. The European Baptist Federation recorded only 4 Baptist churches with 350 members in 1990. Five years later, the number had doubled. By 2002, the statistics registered about 2,500 members in nearly 100 churches and church plants.

From big churches to small churches, rich churches to poor churches, stable churches to persecuted churches, multiplication is a possibility within reach.

Spirit-led risk taking

We need to keep taking risks if our churches are going to be healthy and continue to multiply. A continued outward focus is essential. Consider this testimony from a planter who became a parent church pastor:

> As a new church planter, reaching the 200-attendance mark was an insurmountable goal in my mind. I remember when we reached that point. I was sitting in my office on Monday morning with the little piece of paper in my hand that said there were 206 people in attendance. Wow, I couldn't believe it. I was almost gloating. I actually thought to myself: "We have arrived." My next thought was, "I want to rest now. I want to relax. I've been pushing and working and pushing and working, and now it's my time to rest."
>
> Then the Lord tapped me on the shoulder, and his voice was very distinct. He said, "How many people were in church yesterday?" "206." "How many people weren't in church yesterday?" Within a 20-minute drive of our church there were 200,000 people. I realized then that we weren't even close to being done yet. That moment protected

me and our church from getting stuck right where we were. What I decided that morning was to never be comfortable. We crafted a value statement for our church to live on the edge. We decided that if we ever got to the place where we felt like we'd arrived, that was the moment our church would start to die.

We had to take risks at the beginning of our church plant: huge, irrational steps of faith. When you're just starting out you have to do that. But now with 200 in attendance we didn't have to risk as much anymore. We were doing pretty well with a difficult ministry focus group and nobody would have blamed us if we'd just stayed there and kept doing what we'd been doing. But instead we chose to keep pressing forward and taking risks that we didn't have to take. One of the keys to health is to operate like you do when you're first getting started. If a church ever loses that edge of taking risks, they're going to become a church that needs to be revitalized. Taking risks keeps churches alive.

What makes the difference between a church plant and a church multiplication movement? The second generation. And the third and the fourth. New churches must stay engaged in the planting process if multiplication is going to become a reality. Not only is that involvement necessary for subsequent generations of churches, but the health and vitality of the parent church depends on it.

Stay on track. Remember—As a long-time multiplication movement leader put it, "You're not successful when you have a daughter church—you're successful when you have a granddaughter church."

Next steps

So what now? You've heard the case for church multiplication and want to move forward. You're ready to move on to the second half of this book, where the ten essential aspects of a church multiplication movement are described. My desire in this next section is to give you a beginning framework for moving forward by laying out the next steps in each of the ten essential areas.

But you and I both know that the material in this book isn't nearly enough for you to get a movement up and running—it's just the tip of the iceberg. You're right—you need people. God never intended for us to build his church alone. Start by joining or forming a learning community where you can learn and grow with other like-minded people, a place where you can ask questions, be challenged, and be held accountable. Contact a coach who can walk with you through the process. You can find a coach by visiting *www.coachnet.org*.

To fulfill the great commission, we need to stop doing ministry by addition and start doing ministry by multiplication... planting churches that plant churches that plant churches that plant churches.

"All authority in heaven and on earth has been given to me. Therefore go and make disciples of all nations, baptizing them in the name of the Father and of the Son and of the Holy Spirit, and teaching them to obey everything I have commanded you. And surely I am with you always, to the very end of the age."

Do you want to be a part of that? I do. If you want to be a part of a significant movement of God—move on to part two of this book. Start taking steps toward a multiplication movement. There are plenty of additional resources to help guide you. You may be far away now from where you want to be—that's okay—but start taking steps now. Multiplication is the normal, natural outworking of the church—the way God intended the church to function.

PART TWO

Getting it off the ground

Why strategy?

Introduction

"By wisdom a house is built, and through understanding it is established; through knowledge its rooms are filled with rare and beautiful treasures. A wise man has great power and a man of knowledge increases strength; for waging war you need guidance, and for victory many advisers," says Proverbs 24:3-6. Like the house described in this passage, building a successful church multiplication movement is no small feat—it requires all of those same qualities: wisdom, understanding, knowledge, guidance, and many advisers. Solid planning on the front end can make the difference between unchanneled momentum that fades away and a lasting church multiplication movement.

Within some Christian circles, planning is viewed with suspicion, or even considered unspiritual: "God's plans are higher than ours—he is in control and is powerful enough to accomplish his will. He is the one who brings renewal and revival—not us." As true as that is, it's only one side of the story. The question remains: will we cooperate with what God is doing? Are we positioned to take full advantage of the opportunities he provides?

When Hudson Taylor was back from his first term as a missionary in China and struggling with what God would have him do, he heard this hymn in an English church. "Walk, walk ye winds the story..." the idea being that winds are going to carry the gospel to the rest of the world. And Hudson Taylor cried, "The winds are never going to take the story—people are!"

Another missionary, William Carey, came out of a church that took God's side of the divine-human partnership to the extreme. They said, "Oh, of course God wants to bring people of other nations and other lands to himself. But he will save the heathen in his own time and in his own way." This rationalization got them neatly off the hook. If God is going to do it in his own time and own way, then you don't need to do anything. When Carey suggested founding a mission society, he was told by a pastor, "When God chooses to convert the heathen, he'll do it without the likes of you or me." Experiences such as these led Carey to write a booklet titled: *An inquiry into the obligation of Christians to use means for the conversion of the heathens*.

"Use means," means taking specific steps to see something happen. For Carey, that became forming a mission society. For us, "using means," allows us to create structures and position ourselves so we can most effectively cooperate with what God is doing.

A spontaneous work of God... Structured

As described in the first half of this book, a church multiplication movement means not just starting churches, but starting churches that start churches that start churches that start churches. That's what's necessary to cultivate church multiplication movements that sweep across the globe.

Yet isn't that rather presumptuous? What makes us think we could start such a movement? When we see movements like that, they are obviously such clear works of God in which he pours out his Spirit and brings revival. When speaking in Denmark a few years ago, Dr. Martin Robinson, British church growth expert and historian, said that England has experienced two great revivals: the Wesleyan revival and the Welsh revival. The leaders of Welsh revival refused to organize what was happening because they thought it was unspiritual, and the movement quickly died out. Wesley, on the other hand, recognized what God was doing and channeled it. The result was the Methodist movement, which swept England, the United States, and the world for over 100 years.

It's possible for the Spirit of God to be poured out and for the harvest to be squandered. That's the lesson of Welsh revival. Structure can make the difference between a lasting church multiplication movement and a temporary revival that dies out. The Spirit of God is the primary component, but God calls us to become active participants in his work. Wesley was not unspiritual; he obediently came along behind what God was doing and empowered ordinary people to carry on the work of the gospel. The spiritual and the practical are both essential.

The intent of the second half of this book is to help you get started laying the foundations for a successful church multiplication movement and to get you connected with the resources you'll need to go further. In the following chapters, I'll walk you through the ten essential areas of a church multiplication movement and give you some basics for getting started in creating movements that are structured, reproducible, and Spirit-led.

Proven strategy

Before we get started though, let's look at a few groups that are on the path to church multiplication. I strongly believe that we can learn much from the stories of others. Although there are few full-blown multiplication movements today in the world, a lot of people are on the journey. Some groups are well advanced and others are just beginning the process, but by examining what others have done and highlighting the areas where they are doing well, we can learn a great deal and accelerate our own results.

In the 1980s, one denomination started only 32 new churches and had a 33% survival rate. In 1986, they made a decision not to plant any more churches and were plateaued at 280 churches. In 1990, their national church planting committee began exploring the issue. At one of their conferences, a speaker brought a prophetic word: "You call yourself a missionary church, but you don't care about the person across the street."

That statement caused much anger and some repentance. A number of senior pastors present at the conference began to seek God's forgiveness and confess their sin. They started to refocus again on planting churches. Behind the scenes, the national church planting committee had set a goal of seeing 150 new churches planted during the 1990s. God blessed their efforts, and they saw 180 new churches planted. By adopting reproducible systems and applying a number of the principles found in this book, the survival rate for those churches has gone from 33% to 84%—with a success rate of over 90% for those plants adopting all of the basic systems of a multiplication movement. The final chapters aren't yet written, but this denomination is taking steps in the right direction.

Another denomination began the process of creating a reproducible system for their own ministry context. Through a series of cluster consultations, they developed a national focus and a strategy for empowering their district teams. They have begun to see the implementation of systems and the changing of vocabulary and outlook. The original churches involved in the process are larger and healthier, planting has shifted from addition to multiplication, and they have begun to multiply districts. During a six-year period, they went from a 35% success rate in their church plants to an 87% success rate, climbing as high as 96% in some districts.

And they are still continuing the journey: they now have a vision that includes the planting of 3,000 new churches and have begun the process of developing a comprehensive set of reproducible tools and processes that will integrate their coaching, seminars, training, cluster groups, and resourcing. The end product will be a seamless, customized system that is completely compatible with their philosophy and style of ministry, yet integrates them with the Internet and its resources.

Leaders in this denomination have even begun to pray about whether God will release some of their apostolic leaders to leave and start new denominations. That kind of prayer touches the heart of the Father. Most denominations start by accident. How much more blessing there would be if we recognized those whom God has gifted and freely release them to advance the Kingdom.

These are just two examples of groups that are on a journey. My desire in writing this portion of this book is to give Christian leaders some insights into what I've seen in my work with other groups and to help them to see how the ten essential areas of a healthy church multiplication movement fit together in a holistic system that will dramatically increase the fruitfulness of their ministry.

No matter where you are along the path of development, you can significantly increase fruitfulness by being intentional, deliberate, and focused. Take the next step and grasp the vision for multiplication. My prayer is that this book will whet your appetite for more.

The C2M2 Network

Cultivating Church Multiplication Movements (C2M2))

The Cultivating Church Multiplication Movements (C2M2) Network's interactive resource was created to aid the process of multiplying churches across the face of the globe. C2M2 helps leaders facilitate intentional church multiplication within denominations, church associations, and apostolic networks. Employ a systems approach to church multiplication, and you can foster the development of catalytic leaders and catalytic communities of disciples who will impact their region or people group for Christ. Simple, straightforward, and reproducible, the intentional process embodied within C2M2 has proven an effective method for developing multiplying movements.

While C2M2's approach is intentional and strategic, it doesn't preclude the multiplication process from being relational, organic, and open to the guidance of the Spirit. Leaders are encouraged to factor in the personal and environmental issues that will effectively contextualize the method, for the multiplication process was designed to be wrapped in the natural context of relationship and culture as it is applied.

The C2M2 resource is comprised of ten sections. Building on the material you read in this book, each section represents a key area essential to overall effectiveness, and contains coaching guides, activity sheets, reflections questions and checklists to aid you in developing and strengthening your church multiplication movement. The associated media referenced in each section can be downloaded from the CoachNet® website at *www.coachnet.org*.

C2M2 readers can join the receive a CD and join the Network for $195. Call 1.888.312.7920 or email coachnet@coachnet.org to learn more.

Chapter One

Spiritual dynamics for church multiplication movements

Cultivating a spiritual atmosphere

If Christian leaders hope to plant churches that plant churches that plant churches, the very first step needs to be cultivating a spiritual atmosphere in our churches. All the strategy in the world cannot create a successful church multiplication movement apart from the power of the Holy Spirit. Only through his presence in our churches will people's hearts be opened to hear what God has for them.

Acts 2 describes the spiritual atmosphere of a healthy, growing, multiplication movement: "Everyone was filled with awe" (v. 43a) and "praising God and enjoying the favor of all the people" (v. 47b). Luke paints the picture of a church charged with an atmosphere of growth and openness, a church unafraid of change, a church willing to take great risks to see the gospel spread and the kingdom of God furthered.

Some positive indicators of a growing spiritual atmosphere include:

- Greater enthusiasm and passion for God
- Increase in faith and expectancy
- Greater interest in prayer and intercession
- Spiritual life of leaders deepening - more time spent in prayer and the Word
- Increased number of effective intercessors
- People showing an eagerness in sharing their faith
- Increase in new converts
- Greater cooperation between pastors and churches

- Greater cooperation between churches and other ministries
- Increased awareness of unreached ministry focus groups in your target areas

Many Christian leaders are likely to feel discouraged as they look over this list of characteristics—there's a significant gap between most of our churches and the church in Acts 2. But although it's sometimes painful, taking an honest look at the spiritual atmosphere of our churches will yield much fruit. Evaluating churches to pinpoint areas that need to be addressed can provide a useful starting point for change.

Discerning and addressing spiritual blockages

As any church leader can tell you, the kind of spiritual atmosphere described above doesn't just happen automatically. Creating a church environment that actively fosters and promotes multiplication movements requires some intentional effort. The first step toward spiritual readiness for multiplication is identifying blockages.

Some of the most common blockages that are encountered include:

- Critical attitudes
- Selfish use of resources
- Territorialism
- A fear of losing people
- Apathy
- A maintenance mindset
- Lack of faith or commitment
- A group's theology or ecclesiastical structures
- A competitive rather than cooperative attitude

When asked what was the most common obstacle to spiritual readiness for church multiplication, one church planter responded, "Entrenched religious satisfaction. Many churches just don't see the need to reach new people. They get a little group and become satisfied.

Other churches are just worn out from trying to find a way to reach lost people. I've had conversations with pastors who have told me, 'You know what—I'm just going to minister to Christians rather than trying to engage the culture.' They're just tired of the battle." These pastors need to engage their intercessors until they have won through just as Moses was spiritually supported by Aaron and Hur until victory was gained. (Exodus 17:12)

A congregation was on the verge of a potential church split. A popular associate pastor was leaving over a conflict with the senior pastor, and it looked like about 40% of the members were going with him. The senior pastor took the unprecedented step of embracing the associate pastor and releasing people to go with his blessing. The senior pastor told the associate pastor, "Never make people choose between us. Always make them choose Jesus. It's not my church anyway. It belongs to Jesus. If I can help see new churches planted, I'll give you anyone who wants to go with you." That senior pastor turned a church split into a church plant. He turned an ugly situation around and made it positive. By embracing his associate pastor as a planter, it became a win-win situation. About 20% of the congregation ended up leaving the mother church and both churches kept growing.

Most barriers, whatever their nature, ultimately boil down to a lack of compassion for the harvest. Where true compassion exists, people find ways to overcome any number of obstacles. As a leader, it's up to you to cast vision among the churches you oversee. Find ways to help them see that there's so much more God has for them. Once they recognize on a deep, personal level that the mission of the church is not to be a fortress of refuge, but to reach people who may otherwise never hear the gospel of grace, then church multiplication becomes a reality.

Deepening leaders' prayer lives

Leaders need to model a developing prayer life and actively encourage it in their followers. Although prayer is a challenging area to measure, ways of gauging both frequency and effectiveness do need to be developed. How many church planters, pastors, and denominational leaders have moved forward on the assumption that prayer is happening, only to have effort after effort defeated by the enemy? Prayer is too essential to be left to chance. Look for specific behaviors that indicate the depth and regularity of your leaders' prayer lives.

- How much time is dedicated to praying for church multiplication?
- How much time is devoted to corporate prayer?
- How often do you hear people discussing prayer as a priority in their own lives?
- To what degree are pastoral leaders and potential planters modeling prayer as a priority?
- How much value do they place on the intercessors in their sphere of influence?

Senior pastoral leaders and potential church planters need to be directly involved in praying both individually and with their group or congregation. Prayer cannot become a delegated activity. People look to their leaders to discern priorities, and if they don't see their leaders praying they're likely to assume that prayer isn't that important. They will also take note of the value their leaders place on prayer—often indicated by a willingness to share prayer requests and answers to prayer, and public affirmation of intercessors and the importance of their role. Actions such as these on the part of leaders will feed a greater desire to grow and persist in prayer.

That said, the whole burden of prayer support should not fall on the shoulders of the pastoral leaders. Each planter, apostolic pastor, and denominational leader needs to have a prayer team surrounding and supporting them. This concept is well developed by C. Peter Wagner in his book "*Prayer Shield*". Although they should pray themselves—and will need to in order to be effective in ministry—they should also not be expected to carry it all personally. Intercession is a heavy burden. When leaders allow themselves to need the support of others and be cared for in prayer, they become a more connected part of the whole body of Christ.

In addition to personal prayer, corporate prayer times also serve a crucial function. They promote spiritual unity before the Father and serve to build a strong, united front against the forces of darkness.

As leaders make plans to increase prayer time personally and corporately, they need to think long term and strategically. As one church planting couple was forming their core team, they built an hour a day of mandatory prayer time into their weeklong core team training. That decision served to solidify the commitment to prayer and establish prayer as a central value from the beginning.

Mobilizing strategic intercessors

Mobilizing intercessors must necessarily follow denominational procedures, but asking key sympathetic pastors to enlist their intercessors is usually a good way to start. Most pastors, if given time, can identify the intercessors in their congregations. Even small churches generally have a number of prayer warriors.

Continued mobilization of recruited intercessors consists of regular communication of needs, exposure to the needs of the harvest, further training opportunities, and the encouragement to mentor others. Many intercessors, perhaps because of the nature of their gifting, have not considered the importance of mentoring others in this area, but they generally respond well to the suggestion that they do so. With a little investigation, leaders should be able to identify consistent, committed intercessors—these are the people you want mentoring others.

All aspects of a church multiplication movement need to multiply, and intercessors are no exception.

In addition to recruiting and multiplying intercessors, multiplication movement leaders must develop a strategy for linking intercessors with specific planters. Publicize projects through newsletters (both paper and electronic), email broadcasts to recruited intercessors of new planting projects, offer password-protected websites regularly updated with new project information, denominational publications, area-wide publications, and prayer rallies. Creativity goes a long way towards mobilizing intercessors effectively.

Communicating with intercessors

Planters and multiplication movement leaders are busy people. Yet they cannot afford to neglect prayer or communication with their intercessors. Most planters or project leaders should aim for at least monthly communication with their intercessors.

In communicating prayer needs it's important to communicate from the heart, as intercession has a strong heart component to it. Failure to create real understanding of prayer needs will hamper effective prayer. Giving intercessors specific requests and feedback on answered prayer are keys to helping intercessors feel fulfilled in their ministry and keeping them committed and focused in their prayer efforts.

One pastor sends out weekly email to all of his intercessors. Every time he includes personal stories of things that are happening, ties them to a specific scripture or spiritual principle, then offers a short list of specific prayer requests.

When sharing requests and updates, leaders should note that what is communicated to an inner circle of personal intercessors might be quite different from information given to those praying for the project. A much more intimate relationship, including more down-to-earth communication, will be developed with those intercessors devoted to praying for the planter and his family. Often a partner or close associate can be an excellent liaison between a leader and personal intercessors. They may be more aware of the spiritual attack on family and ministry and may prove to be the best link pin in the process of communication with the personal intercession team.

On the other end, those intercessors praying for the project will need detailed information on how the vision is working itself out, as well as prophetic words, scriptures, and dreams to get their intercessory juices flowing. Some of this will happen naturally as leaders share out of their relationship with God. However, it's unwise to assume that planters will facilitate the flow of communication to their intercessors. Often another member of the church multiplication team can be assigned to oversee this critical area. Consider training not only church planters and their teams, but also others in your group (e.g. key lay leaders in sponsoring churches) in the area of communicating prayer needs and victories. Means of communication are manifold in today's electronic age. The wise leader will use as many methods as possible to facilitate communication.

Whenever possible, those committed to praying should team up at regular intervals for united prayer. Frequency of prayer team meetings will be determined to some extent by logistical factors, but ultimately will be based on the needs of the planters and planting projects. Sometimes planters need extra prayer support at critical times. On such occasions, bringing intercessors together for united prayer can be especially effective.

In addition to communicating prayer needs for movement leaders, intercessors also need to be kept in touch with the needs and spiritual blockages of the focus group. God has a redemptive purpose for each target region or group; that purpose needs to be identified and God's will prayed into the community. Effective prayer requires identifying spiritual strongholds that work against God's redemptive purpose. Praying on site often brings insight. Researching the history of an area, both remote and recent, can bring to light spiritual strongholds and principalities in the target group. Take time also to observe repeated behavior and ingrained thinking in the target populace. These patterns provide clues to underlying strongholds that resist the gospel.

Integrating prayer into all systems

Our natural temptation is to compartmentalize. We end up having the prayer ministry in one space and our other ministries in their own separate spaces. Yet prayer cannot be done effectively in isolation—it needs input from the other systems, and it in turn affects those other systems. It undergirds all ten key areas of church multiplication:

- Spiritual dynamics
- Shared vision
- Planning for church multiplication
- Mobilizing church planters
- Developing church planters
- Assessing church planters
- Coaching church planters
- Parenting new churches
- Developing multiplying networks
- Funding a church planting movement

Paul admonished Timothy to have the church offer up all kinds of prayer for all people (1 Timothy 2:1). Everyone and everything needs a prayer covering. In some cases, different prayer teams can be raised up to cover different facets of the multiplication movement. Not all of these teams can be made up only of gifted intercessors, as prayer is the responsibility of all and intercessors will need to be kept on the cutting edge.

Expanding prayer through new churches

Whatever you do, you always want to increase the capacity so multiplication can continue. As ministry increases, the prayer base needs to increase proportionately, otherwise it will be stretched too thin. Encourage intercessors to pray that more intercessors be raised up to pray for the new churches being planted.

Be intentional about birthing and increasing prayer inside the churches that are planted. Church planters who have mobilized effective prayer efforts are often a great resource in helping other planters do the same. Those who have started prayer teams will have many convincing stories of prayer's positive effect upon their church planting efforts.

Once I was talking with a strongly gifted intercessor, and I asked her for her thoughts on developing a strategy to integrate prayer and church multiplication. She said something that was at once quite obvious and quite profound: "Prayer strategy needs to be birthed in prayer. Don't just start planning a prayer strategy—pray and ask God to show you the prayer strategy."

The revealed strategy needs to be in place early in the history of the multiplication movement. Effective intercession must include teaching on the relationship between leaders and intercessors. The intercessors need their role clearly defined, knowing where their responsibility begins and ends so they do not find themselves trying to control the role of the leader. Leaders need to be strong in their leading and intercessors need to be humble and devoted in their calling.

"Prayer is not preparation for the battle, prayer is the battle." —E.M. Bounds

---

Nothing should be allowed to derail the commitment to having every church planter supported by prayer teams. Some planters may find it easy to put off prayer activities in the midst of all the other things that are going on in a church plant, but they should be encouraged to prioritize prayer above all else. Mobilizing prayer should be approached with more seriousness than any other aspect of church planting. The early church was birthed in prayer and sustained in prayer. As we read in Colossians 1:9, "For this reason, since the day we heard about you, we have not stopped praying for you and asking God to fill you with the knowledge of his will through all spiritual wisdom and understanding." Dare we expect today's church to thrive on any less?

Expanding the prayer base

Before the prayer base can be effectively expanded throughout a church multiplication movement, good foundations need to be laid:

- An effective prayer life for leaders, supported by a team of faithful intercessors

- Freedom from ecclesiastical hindrances to church planting and multiplication in—leaders and workers

- Progress in dealing with barriers in the target community

- A clear understanding of the role of the intercessors to avoid conflict down the road

Once the foundations are in place, where do you start when addressing the need for expanded prayer? Start with what's already being done. Even in cases where there isn't much prayer currently going on, take heart—church multiplication efforts take a quantum leap forward when that most essential ingredient is added. Whatever has been done in the past, plans from this point on can serve to increase prayer greatly. Current estimates put the number of intercessors at about 10% of all Christians, so share the vision, call them out, motivate them, train them, and release them

Events and activities need to be tailored to particular regions and groups, but there are always ways to assemble people for prayer. Usually, at least a few regularly scheduled events are required. The timing of these events is crucial, so think through carefully not only their content but also when they will take place. The following are just a few of the ideas multiplication movement leaders have found useful in expanding their prayer base:

Individual prayer: The prayer of a righteous man availeth much. Mobilizing prayer for church multiplication movements starts with you. How and when will you give yourself to prayer for new churches? Some pray for cities or regions, some pray for specific individuals and teams, some pray for resources and leaders, and some pray for specific systems.

Prayer teams: Small or large teams can meet together or commit to pray individually. Try mobilizing a variety of regional teams, specific projects teams, and personal teams.

Prayer walks: Prayer walking creates intentional opportunities to walk and pray through specific communities where new churches will be planted with an eye for specific needs, opportunities, and insights. This approach can be modified to pray for whole districts and regions.

Concerts of Prayer: Intentional regional gatherings can focus on extended prayer for new church development. Be sure to focus prayer on the harvest, not just the team.

Prayer summits: Prayer summits or retreats gather believers from a particular region to pray for the churches and the harvest. Summits that involve pastors and leaders from a variety of churches in the region promote unity, change lives, release God's power, and overcome strongholds of evil.

Prayer partners: When two or three agree together in prayer, God is there. Prayer partnerships between planters and with pastors and coaches create a web of ongoing prayer in the movement.

Spiritual Mapping: Spiritual mapping is a research activity that discerns the spiritual climate in a given region to identify specific spiritual strongholds that can be prayed through by trained intercessors.

Prayer Clocks: Twenty-four hour prayer clocks can be used to schedule continuous intercession during special times of need.

Prayer Calendars: Printed calendars with specific prayer needs identified can be used to mobilize large amounts of decentralized prayer.
Calendars also have the ability to provide both focus and diversity for
intercessors.

Day/Night of Prayer: Specific extended periods of prayer can focus
both attention and spiritual power on a church multiplication movement or specific needs within that movement. This activity is useful for
seeking vision or attacking a specific stronghold of evil.

Even the smallest church has some intercessors, so start with them.
Finding those called to be intercessors and equipping them with information
related to church multiplication will undergird your efforts with the best
possible support. Identify those with a heart for prayer who are also gifted in
mobilizing and organizing. Since you will always need more intercessors
than you have, equip those who are gifted in raising up other intercessors.
The apostle Paul found it wise to solicit more and more prayer. "Pray also for
me, that whenever I open my mouth, words may be given me so that I will
fearlessly make known the mystery of the gospel, for which I am an ambas-
sador in chains. Pray that I may declare it fearlessly as I should." (Ephesians
6:19-20)

Conclusion

The power of prayer leads to the power of God being unleashed in
ministry.

Robert and Grace Wilder, son and daughter of Royal Wilder, missionary to India in the 19th century, dedicated themselves to praying that God
would raise up new leaders for a church multiplication movement. While a
student at Princeton in 1885, Robert felt God's leading to start a prayer
meeting. He and some other students met daily at noon and for an extended
period on Sunday afternoon for prayer. Grace prayed alone in a separate
room, as was the custom at the time. Grace and Robert prayed and asked
that 1,000 volunteers be secured to labor in foreign fields. God answered
that prayer 20 times over, sending 20,000 people overseas during what later
became known as "the student volunteer movement."

Prayer is God's idea, and he will guide you toward increased effectiveness if you are open. Be thorough and ruthless in your evaluation of your
current prayer efforts. Describe how prayer is being utilized in each area of
your ministry. The keys to improvement are honest evaluation and confident
faith that God can lead us to a better plan. Be sure to look at the positive as
well as the negative. Almost all groups have some areas where they are

seeing effective prayer, and those areas serve not only as encouragement but also as models. What can you learn from areas and instances in which prayer is obviously being effective?

Once the analysis has been completed, delineate plans for increasing prayer effectiveness, without forgetting to "pray about prayer." It's amazing to see how many times we try to improve upon things divine by mere human effort. As the disciples said to Jesus after watching him pray, "Lord, teach us to pray just as John taught his disciples" (Luke 11:1).

Short checklist

Use the following checklist to evaluate the overall health of the spiritual dynamics of your church multiplication movement. You will find the checklist more helpful if in addition to checking off certain areas, you respond in detail as needed. Any areas that you cannot check off should be incorporated into your future planning exercises (we assume that you and your team are familiar with effective planning models. CompuCoach On-line contains some helpful material if you need a review).

INTERCESSORS RECRUITING AND MENTORING OTHER INTERCESSORS

- A strategy that encourages existing intercessors to mobilize other intercessors has been developed.
- Several key intercessors that we can encourage to mentor others have been identified.
- Adequate resources have been collected and made available to intercessors who are mentoring others.

TRAINING OPPORTUNITIES THAT ARE AVAILABLE FOR INTER-CESSORS

- Existing training opportunities to which we can send intercessors have been discovered, and concrete plans have been made to send them to these events.
- Our own training opportunities for intercessors are under development.
- A working method for making books and other resources available to our intercessors has been developed.

LINKING INTERCESSORS WITH PLANTERS OR PROJECTS

- A functional strategy for matching intercessors with planters and projects has been devised.

- A means for ensuring that each planter has a prayer team praying for him/her has been developed.

- A means for encouraging our church planters to develop and nurture their own prayer support with accountability built in has been developed.

Chapter Two

Shared vision for church multiplication movements

Developing a heart for the harvest

As you strive to build shared vision for a church multiplication movement, keep compassion for the lost in the forefront of your vision and strive to develop that compassion in others. Most of us have met people and experienced events that have heightened our sensitivity to the plight of those without Christ. Draw on those experiences in seeking to increase compassion in others. Network with others, especially those with a gift and heart for evangelism, to discover resources designed to increase compassion for the lost.

Turn to the scriptures as well; the wise application of appropriate biblical passages will stir up desire to reach the lost in both church planters and their supporters. God's Word never loses its power when presented with accuracy and clarity. The example of Jesus is powerful: "When he saw the crowds, he had compassion on them, because they were harassed and helpless, like sheep without a shepherd. Then he said to his disciples, 'The harvest is plentiful but the workers are few. Ask the Lord of the harvest, therefore, to send out workers into his harvest fields'" (Matt. 9:36-38).

Emotions are not wrong. Many western cultures tend to be too cerebral, avoiding all appeals to emotion. Yet our emotions are a legitimate and important part of us as human beings. Even a cursory glance at the Psalms confirms that. As we approach developing a shared vision for church multiplication, we need to take a biblical, holistic view of human nature. We are heart, mind, and soul—and we are called to love God with all the facets of who we are. Caring about the harvest serves as the impetus from which vision and action arise, and will ultimately become the driving force behind meeting felt needs in the harvest.

A new church plant in a poor area found that when they did outreach events, kids would show up at the church hungry. In response, they began a ministry called "supper church," where they would feed the people who came. That recognition of the needs in the community ultimately led to a food pantry ministry and to a busing ministry for those who had no transportation to get to church.

In other cases, felt needs will be less obvious, but a caring heart will be able to discern them. A church planter targeting a largely Mormon community found that his ministry focus group often had felt needs similar to those of Christians. One of the most successful outreach events they did was bringing in Josh McDowell for a parenting seminar. Working together with other Christian churches in the area, they built a coalition of resources and participation. They held the event on neutral territory at a local high school and brought in 1,200 people. Because the multiplication movement leaders in that region cared about and understood the needs of their ministry focus group, they were able to do meaningful work in that community.

Regardless of the ministry focus group chosen or its location, caring and wise discernment of their needs will be a key factor in reaching that community. Felt needs offer an emotional bridge into the lives of those in the ministry focus group. Although each community will have some unique needs, many needs transcend community boundaries. If your group has been successful in meeting certain types of needs in other areas, you may be able to meet those same needs in similar ways in newly targeted areas. Yet beware of a "cookie cutter" approach. Do your homework first to ensure that the needs are similar and that they can be met effectively by previously used methods. Work to build relationships also with other churches and agencies in the area to help you accurately discern and meet the real needs of the community.

Identifying the harvest

Consider possible locations and ministry focus groups for each of your church planting efforts. Since your group cannot realistically reach everybody, it's essential for you to narrow your focus to specific target groups that you believe God wants you to reach. If you try to reach everybody, you'll end up reaching nobody. Choosing a specific ministry focus group doesn't create exclusiveness, since "whosoever will" may come. It simply allows energy and effort to be channeled in a clear, focused direction.

The selection of ministry focus groups generally falls into one of three categories: current effectiveness, opportunities, and potential.

Where are we effective? One movement is particularly good at multiplying churches in rural areas. They understand the people and their culture and have adapted their approach to speak effectively to that particular group. Even though they are spreading geographically, enough cultural similarities exist in the population that movement leaders can continue using the same methods to good effect. They know this group of people, they're good at reaching them, and God is blessing their endeavors.

Where are the opportunities? Next, look for opportunities. What people groups are particularly receptive? Where are people more open to the message of the gospel? In many cases, immigrant populations that have recently relocated demonstrate great receptivity. Other times opportunities are discovered during the course of ministry. A young apostolic pastor was working in a lower socioeconomic area. In identifying effective ways to reach out to lower income people generally, he realized one of the most receptive subsets of that group was students at the local university. The pastor and his team began meeting some practical felt needs, then moved into pastoring, mothering, and fathering these young students. Numbers responded to Christ and the pastor is now looking to plant a church among the university students with an eye toward continued multiplication as the student population graduates and relocates.

Where do we have the potential to expand? It's also helpful to ask where your movement has the potential to expand. As mentioned earlier, most evangelical churches are located within driving distance of unchurched communities. Having daughter churches nearby can be a big support in terms of prayer, encouragement, and ministry.

Clarifying vision and values

A vision for the kind of churches that need to be planted spring from underlying values, and those values must be rooted in scripture. The preparation of a biblical argument for church multiplication will help get other believers on board. Sincere Christians respond well when confronted with God's will as it is revealed in scripture. Even more important than getting others on board, a firm biblical foundation for what we do means that God is on board. Have the courage to evaluate all of your values and vision on the basis of scripture.

Once you are certain of your values, think through carefully how they will function in the field. Biblical values without the means to apply them in real life settings won't be effective. Attach specific behaviors to each value, making it a concrete reality instead of an abstract concept. If something is really a value, it will be demonstrated by behavior. Consider some of your stated values and then ask yourself, "What are some examples of ways we are doing that?" If it really is a value, you'll have no shortage of examples of how it's lived out. In cases where there aren't specific examples, maybe it's a desired value rather than an actual value. The first step toward change is an honest recognition of the gap between where you are and where you'd like to be.

As you move into applying values, consider how out of sync our methods sometimes are with our target audience. More than ever before, our style must match the people we are trying to reach. They will not hear the message if it is not presented in their language. Adapting our style does not mean that we abandon our uniqueness, only that we seek to ensure that our uniqueness is wrapped in an appropriate framework that matches our target group. We must "exegete the culture" in each planting target environment, designing the church the community needs—not just the church the planter desires personally.

Discerning & addressing spiritual blockages

As discussed in the chapter on spiritual dynamics, blockages exist within target groups that must be broken down through prayer. We expect that—after all, unbelievers are in the territory of the enemy and he will not easily let go of his strongholds. Yet we are sometimes less aware of spiritual blockages existing within the body of Christ. These are the blockages in the hearts of God's people that hinder the development of a shared vision for the harvest. Blockages such as these must be discerned and addressed if a vision for church multiplication is to be embraced and sustained in any meaningful way.

"For though we live in the world, we do not wage war as the world does. The weapons we fight with are not the weapons of the world. On the contrary, they have divine power to demolish strongholds. We demolish arguments and every pretension that sets itself up against the knowledge of God, and we take captive every thought to make it obedient to Christ." 2 Corinthians 10:3-5

Where a commitment to church multiplication is lacking, it means that one or more values have been wrongly embraced. If a church truly holds the values of God's kingdom, then a commitment to multiplication would be natural. So what is the hindrance? What values have been wrongly embraced? Finding the answer will require much discernment and prayer. One of the more common examples of a value that has been wrongly embraced is greed as opposed to generosity. Jesus tells us we must lose our life to save it, and that if we try to save our life we will surely lose it. When churches go on the defensive against the world and begin to feel threatened, they often fall prey to a mindset of hoarding resources. The temptation becomes hanging onto people instead of releasing them, and the result is a limited local vision instead of a kingdom perspective.

Check your own heart and your own faith as you put together your case for church multiplication. If you aren't convinced that God is in your plans, you certainly won't be able to convince others. Dealing with the doubts, fears, and excuses in your own heart can help prepare you to deal with them in others.

When presenting a vision for church multiplication, anticipate hindrances that may arise. Each group has its own dynamics related to change and new directions. Knowing where a particular group usually bogs down will help you know how to move constituents past their doubts into faith for the future.

Time spent in prayer and time spent talking to key leaders within the congregation will give you a good idea of the specific spiritual blockages present in each church. Addressing these blockages—lovingly and with scripture—will yield much fruit as you work to develop a vision for church multiplication that is truly shared.

Remember that some people will respond immediately upon hearing your vision, others will come aboard mid-term, others later, and some not at all. Understanding this "adoption curve" can help leaders formulate different responses to each of these groups of people, increasing the chances of the long-term success of the vision. Each group will require a different kind of approach:

- The early adopters need to be folded into the process immediately so they can become involved.

- The midterm adopters need to be constantly encouraged to see the big picture.

- The late adopters require patience and a lot of factual/statistical verification of fruit.

- The non-adopters need to be treated with grace, love, and acceptance.

Communicating vision effectively

Vision must be communicated to others if it is to be effective: "Even in the case of lifeless things that make sounds, such as the flute or harp, how will anyone know what tune is being played unless there is a distinction in the notes? Again, if the trumpet does not sound a clear call, who will get ready for battle?" (1 Corinthians 14:7-8).

Vision becomes contagious when it is communicated clearly and often. With today's many forms of communication, why not expand the number of ways you cast your vision? The more gateways that are used to communicate vision, the more likely it is to strike a resonant chord in the lives of people.

- Newsletters
- Brochures
- Audio tapes
- CDs
- Video tapes
- DVDs
- Websites
- E-newsletters
- Seminars for potential planters and parent church pastors
- Testimonies from planters, parent church pastors, or individuals whose lives have been touched through the ministry of a church plant
- Live music
- Drama
- Poetry
- Readings
- Visual art

When communicated well, vision touches every part of the human being: the mind, the spirit, and the emotions. Creative communication of vision is all around you. Look at some of the ways others are getting their vision across—it may stir up some effective ways to communicate yours.

CASTING VISION AMONG PASTORS

Some pastors and their spouses attended a regional retreat for their denomination. The retreat coordinators passed out 4x6 laminated prayer cards with maps of the region and prayer requests: workers, facilities, spiritual barriers, cross-cultural situations, soil prepared for the seed of the gospel, etc. The pastors and spouses gathered in groups of four, prayed, then exchanged cards with other groups and prayed again. The exercise helped people get a visual picture of the harvest and feel informed about what was going on in church planting and multiplication.

Increasing commitment to multiplication

Actions demonstrate commitment. Church leaders who are truly committed to church multiplication movements don't just talk about it—they demonstrate their commitment in terms of investment: investment of their time, their people, and their resources.

Building that shared vision for church multiplication and increasing the level of commitment can be visualized cyclically. Each step leads into the next, and with each step the momentum increases, resulting in continual improvement: act, reflect, learn, refocus.

Planning Cycle

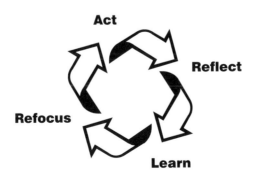

Act

Reflect

Refocus

Learn

Here are some steps to help you increase the commitment to multiplication:

- Assess the current level of commitment (measured behaviorally)
- Identify the blockages
- Pray against spiritual blockages
- Analyze core values that have been embraced
- Address core values
- Act in the opposite spirit to begin changing core values
- Communicate vision for change
- Develop a strategy to increase multiplication
- Identify harvest fields
- Prioritize church plants
- Continue communicating vision

Actions are the outgrowth of underlying attitudes. Wisdom therefore dictates that you look beyond the action for the attitude that is motivating it, whether the action is a positive one you wish to reinforce or a negative one you wish to change. Leaders strongly committed to church multiplication are inevitably motivated by strong compassion for lost people and an unshakeable conviction that the gospel is indeed the power of God for those who believe.

Many times peers are best at motivating peers. If some key leaders under you demonstrate high commitment, point them in the direction of others who also need to embrace the vision. Testimonies from parent church pastors can be particularly powerful.

Short checklist

Use the following checklist to evaluate the overall shared vision of your church multiplication movement. You will find the checklist more helpful if in addition to checking off certain areas, you respond in detail as needed. Any areas that you cannot check off should probably be incorporated into your future planning exercises (we assume that you and your team are familiar with effective planning models.

CompuCoach On-line contains some helpful material if you need a review).

IDENTIFYING HARVEST FIELDS

- Factors to use for considering whom we will reach have been identified (e.g. geography, ethnicity, level of need, etc.).
- Current effectiveness has been determined (e.g. urban, suburban, small town, rural, ethnic group, age group etc.).
- Future locations and ministry focus groups for church planting ventures have prayerfully been determined.
- Plans to identify the needs in the communities we have targeted have been clarified.
- Resources and relationships needed to help us to meet the needs in your target communities have been identified.
- Resources that we can use to increase compassion for the lost have been identified (e.g. scriptures, strategic reading, multi-media presentations, personal testimonies, etc.).

CLARIFYING VISION AND VALUES

- Vision for church multiplication in our region/district has been clarified.
- Uniqueness of our efforts has been stated.
- Appropriate style(s) of church has been determined.
- Biblical mandates have been studied.
- Ministry values and value statements have been clarified.

DISCERNING & ADDRESSING SPIRITUAL BLOCKAGES

- Mindsets, attitudes and excuses in our history that hinder church multiplication have been discerned.
- Strategy for overcoming these mindsets, attitudes and excuses has been developed.
- Spiritual strongholds in the target area have been discerned.
- Intercessors have been mobilized to tear down these spiritual strongholds.

COMMUNICATING VISION EFFECTIVELY

- Methods presently used for vision casting have been evaluated for effectiveness.
- New methods for vision casting have been explored.
- New avenues and venues for vision casting have been explored.

INCREASING COMMITMENT TO MULTIPLICATION

- Actions and attitudes have been articulated that we would like to encourage in leaders that demonstrate commitment to the church multiplication vision.
- Actions and attitudes of leaders have been evaluated for evidence of commitment to the vision.
- Methods for increasing commitment have been evaluated for effectiveness.
- New methods have been considered for increasing commitment.

PRIORITIZING NEW CHURCH PLANTS

- Locations and ministry focus groups have been considered for the next 3-5 years.
- Locations/ministry focus groups have been considered for the next 5-10 years.
- Criteria for prioritization have been articulated.
- Lists of locations/ministry focus groups have been prioritized.

DEVELOPING ACTION PLANS, GATHERING RESOURCES

- Goal and action steps have been written.
- Dates for completion of goals have been determined.
- Personnel responsible for execution have been determined.
- Resources needed have been assessed.
- Plans for gathering those resources have been made.
- Evaluation times have been built into the process.

Chapter Three

Planning for church multiplication

Organizing for the future

John Wesley is a prime example of someone who planned for the future in order to get the most out of what God was doing. He thought ahead and organized to make sure that multiplication was happening at every level. He established circuits at the regional level. These circuits were made up of multiplying small groups called societies that provided pastoral care from trained lay people for basic Christian community. After societies, Wesley felt the need to lower the bar even further. He founded an even smaller multiplying unit called class meetings—something we might call accountability and discipleship groups. Wesley viewed these class meetings as a means of evangelism. In spite of his legendary public preaching itinerary, he believed that it was in these groups that salvation was actually applied to the souls of the converts. In fact, his circuit preachers were not to preach in a place if class meetings were not being formed. He told them, "Preach in as many places as you can. Start as many classes as you can. Do not preach without starting new classes." Preaching was merely a preamble, a means to awaken them to their need for Christ. It was within the relationship of a class meeting that people actually encountered Christ and began their relationship with him.

Solid planning is essential for a sustained church multiplication movement; the strategic groundwork must be laid. This is the task of a church multiplication team: to oversee the development of the movement at every level. An effective system will use intentionality and planning to multiply disciples, groups, churches, and parent churches to the ends of the earth.

Prioritizing new church plants

Most church groups don't have the resources to launch several projects at once, so deciding which ones should receive highest priority and earliest attention is an essential step. After the vision has been clarified and some potential target groups and regions have been brainstormed, leaders will need to prioritize in order to ensure that action takes place in the near future.

It's best to narrow initial possibilities to the top five locations. Prioritizing that list will allow for focus, increasing the likelihood of the initial plants being successful. Such early victories can help build momentum for continued church multiplication. The learning experiences from these plants will also serve to inform future efforts.

Develop criteria to help prioritize projects. With a few initial planting projects in mind, consider important issues such as:

- Available personnel
- Financial resources
- The spiritual health of the parent church/movement
- The extent of existing infrastructure to support the plant
- The depth and breadth of acceptance of the church multiplication vision

Above all, listen to discern the voice of God. "Paul and his companions traveled throughout the region of Phrygia and Galatia, having been kept by the Holy Spirit from preaching the word in the province of Asia. When they came to the border of Mysia, they tried to enter Bithynia, but the Spirit of Jesus would not allow them to. So they passed by Mysia and went down to Troas. During the night Paul had a vision of a man of Macedonia standing and begging him, 'Come over to Macedonia and help us.' After Paul had seen the vision, we got ready at once to leave for Macedonia, concluding that God had called us to preach the gospel to them." Acts 16:6-10

In catalyzing new ventures, church multiplication teams often choose strategic areas where they can have the most influence. By branching off existing churches, teams can often create bridges into unreached territory. Envision starting churches in new cultural groups and new geographical areas. Ed Silvoso, in *That None Should Perish*, suggests that there needs to be one evangelical church for every 1,000 people in a community. In most communities this means the planting of many more churches, so it's unlikely that the opportunities for church plants will be exhausted in the near future. Most areas are under churched. Church multiplication teams need to continually challenge themselves by asking, "How can we continue to expand what we are doing?" With creative thinking, the possibilities are limitless.

Developing action plans, gathering resources

Action planning: Now is the time to lay out a plan with specific, measurable goals and clear steps for achieving those goals. At this point, connection with a good coach is indispensable. When applying strategic planning to a church multiplication vision, keep the following framework in mind:

- Vision
- Goals
- Steps
- Action Items/Individual tasks

All of these must be laid out, placed on a timeline, assigned to individuals, and placed on their calendars. Accountability must remain high in order to avoid being sidetracked by more "urgent" needs.

Planning team: A church multiplication team needs to be formed to facilitate the overall development of the movement. This team should be made up of people with a vision for multiplication, including recent planters and parent church pastors, and should be defined by the region it will be responsible for overseeing. Once formed, this team will need to meet quarterly, or more often in the beginning, with a basic agenda of items to be covered. Part of the agenda for these meetings should be reviewing the master checklist for church multiplication movements. (This is a compilation of the checklists at the end of each of the ten chapters in this part of the book.) Due to the intensive nature of the work, the church multiplication team needs to meet for extended periods of evaluation, refocusing, and creating action plans.

Reproducibility: Any methods you use for planting churches and developing leaders need to be simple enough to be infinitely reproduced, yet effective enough to be worth reproducing. If something is not reproducible and cannot be done by others, it should not be done, as this will directly affect the multiplication aspect. Keep activities, roles and tasks as simple as possible. An "expert system"—one that relies on a few highly skilled and specialized individuals—defeats the multiplication process.

Leadership development: Reproducibility includes the reproduction of leaders. No plan is complete without some provision for the ongoing development of leaders. Considerable thought needs to be expended now as to how people will be discipled and released into leadership.

Permissions: Be certain not to overlook getting the necessary permissions and connecting with the necessary networks within your organization. Every denomination or group has its own means of getting permission. Think through your list carefully so that everyone who needs to be on board is on board from the beginning. Trying to "sell" something later to a key leader who was missed may be hard to do.

Personnel resources: As your plan takes shape, brainstorm a list of the resources you may need. People are your most vital resource. Identify all the roles needed to develop, launch, and maintain your church multiplication systems; be as complete as possible, including supporting personnel as well as primary leaders. Assigning church multiplication system roles based simply on a polity position that an individual may have is a common mistake. Gifting, acceptance of the church multiplication vision, and passion for reaching the harvest through new churches are non-negotiable qualifications. People not holding recognized organizational leadership positions might sometimes be better suited for the roles functionally.

Financial resources: Financial resources will also be needed, but remember that a high financial commitment per church plant may slow things down and also limit your ministry focus groups to higher income people. Utilizing bivocational and volunteer personnel in every aspect of the church multiplication process can help conserve financial resources.

Follow up and review: Once initial plans are laid and strategies are implemented, the system cannot be left to run on autopilot. The church multiplication team will need to review its entire program annually. Quarterly meetings can get bogged down in details, causing people to lose sight of the overall vision and direction. Time will need to be deliberately set aside for such a review, so a comprehensive perspective is not neglected. Some groups opt to set up a separate annual meeting specifically for refocusing the vision, while others build the review into one of their quarterly planning meetings. The latter works well only if a part of the meeting is intentionally and irrevocably set-aside for this purpose.

The following questions may be helpful to use as a framework for the annual review and evaluation of a church multiplication movement:

- What positive changes have we seen in our region due to the church multiplication process?

- What changes are slow in coming and need some focused energy?
- As we review our master plan, what changes, additions, and adjustments need to be made?
- How will we sustain and increase the momentum from the church multiplication process in our region?
- In what ways is the vision still appropriate for our region? What might need adjustment?

Evaluating, improving and multiplying each component

Any good planning strategy begins with an evaluation of the present state of affairs. Asking questions like these can help evaluate each aspect of a church multiplication movement and identify which areas need work:

- Where are we now?
- Which church multiplication dynamics are we strongly implementing?
- Where have we reached our stated goals?
- Where have we not reached our stated goals?
- Where have we made significant progress?

If your team finds itself unable to provide clear answers to these questions, check again to be sure the goals are measurable. Setting measurable goals each time your team meets is one of the best ways to ascertain true progress. However, recognize that some areas where you may have made progress may not be easy to measure objectively. For example, a general positive attitude among churches towards church planting may have increased—something that is hard to measure. In subjective areas like these, there should be consensus by the team members, and attempts should be made to objectify the area in the future (such as measuring positive attitude via a survey).

Once problem areas have been identified, begin looking at possible improvement strategies. The questions below can help facilitate that process:

- What are the limiting factors for multiplying what we are doing?
- What key priorities need to be addressed in the next three to six months?
- What do we need to stop doing, start doing, or continue doing but improve on?

- What measurable goals need to be set for the future?
- What action steps do we need to take?
- What adjustments need to be made to the overall plan?

Establish the priority of action items by identifying the main areas where you have not reached your goals. Next, analyze these areas to see if you can discern obstacles or blockages and develop a plan for removing them. Finally, describe how you will set that area up to expand and multiply. Again, working with a good coach is extremely beneficial in navigating this process.

Completing "reality checks" prior to implementation of a plan can save you a lot of grief later on.

Does your plan have:

• Manageable units?	• Realistic schedule?
• Clear milestones?	• Adequate personnel?
• Gaps identified?	• Sufficient resources?
• Logical sequence?	• Contingency plans?

Some initial success in church planting will almost certainly generate new interest from people in your group or denomination. Make plans now to involve those whose interest has increased because of the effectiveness of what you are doing. However, also recognize that individual regions within your group will probably experience varying levels of success. Be prepared to share both successes and obstacles so districts and regions can learn from one another and provide encouragement for those that are struggling.

Enabling multiplication systems to work together

The more effectively the various parts of a church multiplication system work together, the more effective overall multiplication will be. Interdependence is essential for health. All systems should fit seamlessly together. Spiritual dynamics, for instance, should support all of the rest of the nine components: assessment, coaching, funding, etc. The prayer component should not be done in isolation, but should be integrated throughout the system so information flows smoothly to intercessors.

Regular, clear communication is probably the most important factor in creating smooth interfaces. Although good communication becomes more difficult if the team grows and the volume of information increases, each individual areas must stay connected to the whole. Continue to:

- Listen to one another, attempting to understand not just words but emotions.
- Ask questions that help people talk through what they're thinking or feeling.
- Be willing to learn from other people.
- Be honest about the good and the bad - speak the truth in love.

Clear delineation of responsibility and authority will also help. Someone ministering in the coaching area, for example, must know what specific outcomes they are responsible for and what decisions they have the authority to make.

Everything human can be improved, so seize evidence of breakdowns as opportunities to make something good even better. Encourage lots of honest feedback from those in the system so you can identify and correct breakdowns and incompatibilities.

One team made the discovery that they were training planters but not getting them hooked up well with the coaches. The coaching wasn't working not because the coaches weren't good, but because no relational basis had been built. A disconnect resulted from the planters not knowing the coaches. The team realized they needed to integrate the training system seamlessly into the coaching system, so they decided to get the coaches involved in the training process relationally. The new process provided a better foundation for the coaches and a smoother transition for the planters.

Increasing the number of parent churches

A church multiplication movement should ultimately create not only more new churches, but also more new parent churches. That's where the future potential lies—in making church plants into parent churches. Generally this type of growth is measured by the number of successful church planting efforts by parent churches, but be sure not to overlook failed attempts since even a model system will have some failures.

Take an honest look at the percentage of increase of new churches and of parent churches in your region—a church multiplication movement should cause the percentage of healthy new churches to increase annually. Measuring this growth will provide a good handle on how well a church multiplication movement is working. Unfavorable discoveries in this area should be viewed as opportunities for refocusing and adjustment, not as defeats or insurmountable obstacles. Set goals for the future based on an honest evaluation of the commitment of the pastors in your region to having their churches become parent churches. Hopefully this commitment will increase over time, but preliminary goals should reflect a standard slightly higher than the current level of commitment.

Short checklist

Use the following checklist to plan your church multiplication move-ment. You will find the checklist more helpful if in addition to checking off certain areas, you respond in detail as needed. Any areas that you cannot check off should be incorporated into your future planning exercises.

SCHEDULING QUARTERLY PLANNING MEETINGS

- Dates for the extended planning meetings for the next 18 months have been scheduled.

- Essential people to be at these meetings have been contacted and have put the date on their calendars.

- Responsibilities for these meetings have been delegated.

EVALUATING, IMPROVING AND MULTIPLYING EACH COMPONENT

- Evaluation of our church multiplication process in terms of the accomplishment of stated goals has been accomplished.

- Evaluation of our church multiplication process for needed improve-ments has been done.

- Key priorities that need to be addressed in the next three to six months have been identified.

- Limiting factors for multiplying have been addressed.

ENABLING MULTIPLICATION SYSTEMS TO WORK TOGETHER

- Church multiplication system has been assessed for smooth func-tioning.

- Breakdowns or incompatibilities have been addressed.

- Positive interfacing of various components has been confirmed.

CATALYZING NEW VENTURES

- The need for new churches (geographically or culturally) has been assessed.

- Specific need have been identified in these locations.
- Preliminary research has been carried out.
- Blockages to starting these new churches have been addressed.

REFOCUSING VISION, GOALS AND PLANS ANNUALLY

- Specific quarterly meetings for the purpose of including an annual review have been scheduled.
- These meetings have been given a high level of priority in our schedules.
- Team members have been alerted as to the key questions to be raising about our master plan.

INCREASING THE PERCENTAGE OF NEW CHURCH AND OF PARENT CHURCHES

- Careful analysis in terms of health and growth on the number of new churches started in the last 3-5 years has been done.
- Number of new churches to be started in the next 3 years has been stated.
- Roadblocks to reaching our goals have been noted and addressed.
- Careful analysis on the number of parent churches involved in church planting efforts in the last 5 years has been done.
- Goals for increased participation in the next three years have been stated.

Chapter Four

Mobilizing church planters

Recruiting vs. developing

Leaders are the future of a church multiplication movement. If the leadership is strong, the movement will be strong. Mobilizing church planters who have a vision and a zeal for the harvest is one of the best assurances of the continued progress of the movement.

Some groups try to solve their planter shortage by recruiting qualified planters—maybe implementing some of the material from this chapter. That's a good start, but it's ultimately a short-term fix. Recruiting from a pool of existing planters diminishes that pool, which leads to more shortages down the road. Temporary recruitment success has the inadvertent side effect of short-circuiting long-term development. The more successful a group is at recruiting, the less effort they are likely to put into developing new leaders. And developing new leaders is the long-range solution—it's the only way to increase ministry capacity. Although there will be an initial delay between recruitment and deployment, this strategy avoids leader shortages—the number one blockage identified by Jesus. If we invest in development, the supply of leaders is limitless.

While mobilizing leaders does involve attracting and recruiting qualified planters, it goes well beyond that into the realm of developing new leaders. The whole process could best be described as *discovering leaders*—wherever they are on the continuum of development and experience. This chapter focuses on attracting promising church planter candidates, and the next chapter focuses on how to develop those candidates. However, in reality, both of these processes work in tandem.

Determining the needs

Not surprisingly, a successful multiplication movement requires many workers. As Jesus tells us, "The harvest is plentiful, but the workers are few. Ask the Lord of the harvest, therefore, to send out workers into his harvest field" (Luke 10:1-2). More workers are always needed. Given your particular planting goals and circumstances—how many workers will you need? And what kind of workers?

To determine the number of church planters needed, begin with a realistic projection of the number of church plants envisioned in the next three to five years. This kind of "back planning" or "reverse engineering"—starting with a future goal and working backward to a present reality—allows for a more vision-driven process. Yet be sure the vision is a realistic one. Initial goals should be commensurate with the size and scope of an organization. A district of 20 churches that sets a goal of planting 100 churches in the next three to five years is setting itself up for disappointment and discouragement. Start with small measurable goals; they can always be expanded later after initial success.

At beginning of a church multiplication movement, try to recruit proven church planters with solid track records for being able to catch a vision and carry it out. The stronger start you get, the more momentum you'll have. It's also preferable to get solid commitments at a slower pace than to assume commitment on the basis of a rushed process.

That said, recruitment of current capable planters must coincide with the development of future planters—the subject of the next chapter. Investment in future planters and other leaders and workers is critical to long-term success. Think of recruiting planters as addition and developing new leaders as multiplication. Without new, developing planters, leaders, and workers, a movement will quickly use up all experienced people and will be unable to grow beyond addition to multiplication.

John Wesley discovered this principle at work in his ministry. As people were converted, he folded them into discipling communities where they would be nurtured and challenged to discipleship. When he couldn't find enough ordained clergy for the ministry, Wesley's mother asked him, "John, don't you think God could use laymen?" So he appointed a lay leader for each society to lead, nurture, exercise discipline, and provide spiritual oversight. Many of these leaders served on a trial basis until their leadership ability had been proven. Some went on to become lay preachers. Wesley tried to have his preachers ordained in the Anglican Church but the established clergy was unsympathetic, so he realized the only solution was to continue raising up lay leaders from the harvest. The resulting multiplication led to the development of circuits, the appointment of superintendents to oversee those circuits, and finally to a new movement.

Church multiplication movements today also require a variety of leaders. In addition to planters, consider other roles that will need to be filled. What strategies are in place to mobilize these kinds of leaders?

- Disciple-making leaders who start and multiply cell groups
- Catalytic church planters who start multiple congregations
- Parent church pastors who sponsor new church plants
- Coaches who empower and equip church planters
- Mentors who raise up disciple-making leaders, church planters, and missionaries to start and multiply churches
- Denominational supervisors who provide visionary leadership for starting and multiplying new churches regionally or nationally
- Apostolic leaders who catalyze and/or facilitate regional or national church multiplication movements
- Church planter apprentices who can be teamed up with newly planted churches to help them begin planting more churches

Enhancing attractiveness to planters

To effectively attract church planters and other leaders for a multiplication movement, an organization will need to make itself, its vision, and its process as attractive as possible to potential planters. That attractiveness is based on many things: what you offer, how you communicate and relate to people, and who you are.

Do you offer coaching? Many younger planters today crave mentoring or coaching relationships with experienced planters and pastors. To them, such relationships mean a great deal and can be a significant means of attracting quality young leaders. Other key points may include training opportunities and a long-term commitment to church multiplication. You may have noticed that I haven't mentioned money. Although money plays a part, I believe it is not nearly the determining factor most people assume it is. I personally know many planters who have turned down full financial packages from some denominations to work with other groups that offered a more relational approach. They've chosen to plant on a shoestring budget with organizations that offer vision, support, training, coaching, relationship, and strategy. Those things—much more than money—are the determining factors for most planters.

Recruitment is not an event. It's a relationship—and relationships take time. Take time to listen to the individual's spiritual commitment and calling. Listen to their vision for future ministry as well as sharing your own vision. Meet and get to know their family and some of their friends. Taking the time to invest in relationship will lead to a stronger overall mobilization process.

Every group has strengths, yet honesty requires us to recognize that every group also has areas where improvement is needed. There are some things peculiar to any group that may be hindrances to attracting planters and other leaders. Try to identify specific issues and determine which ones can be changed. Consider what actions you can take to make your church multiplication movement more attractive to planter candidates. Blockages that can be changed should be prioritized in terms of urgency. Blockages that cannot be changed immediately should be committed to long-term prayer. Ask the Lord to remove the blockages, and for wisdom on how to work around them in the meantime.

Eight qualities of an attractive planting movement

Reputation: What is the reputation of your movement? Contemporary? Evangelistic? Growing? What are your distinctives? Theology? Tradition? Ministry?

Vision: Do you have an attractive vision for church multiplication? Does your movement have attractive visionary leadership?

Compassion for lost people: How do you emphasize outreach, compassion ministry and evangelism?

Diversity: Are you prepared to reach the diversity of the harvest and therefore attract a diversity of church planters?

Character: What is the quality and character of your leaders, pastors and people?

Coaching: What kinds of ongoing coaching, training and resources can you provide to the church planting team?

Resources: Do you have reasonable financial resources and benefits to attract the planters you need?

Success: Do you have a track record of successful ministry and church planting?

Consider issues not just related to logistics or practicality, but also matters of style. For example, sincerity and authenticity are essential in attracting younger planters. Too much hype or overselling will repel them.

One organization evaluated themselves for attractiveness to church planters. They recognized that their positives included being seen as stable, well organized, and well run. They also had some specificity regarding their ministry focus group and provided training specifically geared toward reaching that group.

Yet they also recognized that they were sometimes viewed as too stodgy, slow, and programmatic to do pioneer mission church planting. Their tendency toward structure, schedule, and routine has been interfering with recruitment of visionary planters. They've implemented improvements in that area and are moving the whole organization slowly toward a church planting model, but it's been an uphill struggle. As with any major paradigm shift, change takes time. The leadership can turn the steering wheel, but rest of the boat still takes a while to follow suit.

Evaluate your organization thoroughly. What plans do you have to improve? Strategies for removing blockages and enhancing attractiveness need to be just as complete as strategies for highlighting strengths. Plans for change should include prioritized action steps as well as who, what, and when.

Developing materials for attracting planters

- What recruitment tools do you already have available?
- What do you need to develop?
- Examine the look and feel of your promotional material—the information you put into the hands of potential planters. Is it contemporary?
- Does it match the type of people you're trying to attract?
- Does it communicate with people who are in touch with the current world?
- Does it demonstrate an understanding of their perspective?

Sometimes people inquire about becoming a church planter and the denomination sends them a package: the 45 requirements for being a planter, the qualification checklist, the 30 step process for working with our denomination—all laid out in great detail. That type of package can leave a potential planter feeling overwhelmed with information. They walk away thinking, "I have to do all of this on my own. I don't think I can."

Instead, try designing a brochure that provides a basic overview of your organization's vision and process. This approach can help people see the basic pathways to getting where they want to go without burying them in unnecessary detail. Material like this will present a more relational environment, one that invites prospective planters into a dialogue: "Here's what we offer, and here's how to get connected and find out more—call us or drop us an email and we can start talking."

Tools to share with church planting candidates

- Attractive visionary brochure
- Answers to the most frequently asked questions
- Testimony of a successful and satisfied planter
- Top ten reasons to plant with us
- Map of the recruitment, assessment, and placement process
- Attractive, visual information about the communities where you want to plant churches
- Literature, video, and computerized resources

In certain respects, recruiting church planters can be similar to a dating relationship. You talk with a lot of different people, find some you connect with more than others, and start narrowing the field. You take a step toward a person, then they take a step toward you. You don't want to move too fast or you'll frighten them. Just as you wouldn't propose on the first date, you wouldn't send a prospective planter a contract after the first inquiry. On the other hand, you don't want to move too slowly either or you might discourage the other person with a perceived lack of interest.

As you take steps toward church planters and give them time to respond, you might provide certain materials at each stage along the way that would be appropriate for that place in the process. At the beginning, you might give planters a brochure broadly describing your vision and who you are as an organization. Then, if that sounds good to them, make it clear what step they should take next. When they take that step, be faithful to follow up promptly with more information, opportunity for dialogue, and guidance regarding the next stage of the process.

Helpful tips on recruiting material:

- Recruiting tools should culturally match the type of planters you are trying to recruit
- Use a variety of communication methods: email, websites, CDRoms, DVDs, etc.
- Test your materials on your intended audience before producing them en masse. Are you communicating what you intend to communicate?

Finding potential church planters

How do you find potential church planters? When Jesus pointed out the shortage of workers for the harvest to his disciples, his solution was prayer (Matthew 9:37-38). Yet prayer without a willingness to develop strategy cannot be productive. Jesus himself took action after he admonished prayer by sending the twelve into the harvest (Matthew 10:1). Begin with the end in mind. Your recruitment strategy has to be driven by the outcomes you want to see in 3-5 years.

As you begin seeking church planters, keep in mind that they usually do not look like your typical pastor. Expand your horizons in terms of the type of people you consider as potential church planters. Instead of looking for traditional pastor-types, look for two key qualities: people who start things and people who empower others.

Two key qualities: people who start things and people who empower others

---

Cultural environments: One multiplication movement leader tries to stay on the lookout for planters who will fit well in particular environments. One of the planters he recruited was Tyler, a retired pro football player. Tyler left seminary after one year, but then intentionally moved his family to a low-income urban neighborhood and began working with some of the local football teams. Tyler is absolutely not a typical church planter, yet he is a person very deeply committed to church multiplication within his chosen community.

Age: Be sure not to rule out the young—especially if your group does not require formal theological training for planting ministry. Yet even when that training is required, sometimes creative work-arounds for planter recruitment can be found.

One day two of Russian immigrants wandered into a Russian language Bible study class with four people in it. The class was being offered by a multicultural church. In that setting, these two Russian immigrants discovered that the yearnings they had as children were a call to ministry, but when they were children in the Soviet Union there wasn't anybody to tell them that. They immediately enrolled in seminary. One of the pastors asked them, "What if we were to help you through seminary and—while you get acquainted with Christianity and with our denomination—you lead this Bible study? Then when you finish seminary, we'll help you start a Russian immigrant church."

They agreed to the plan and started leading the Russian Bible study, but they didn't wait for graduation to begin forming a core for their new church. Within four months of becoming Christians, they began to grow a congregation from that Bible study. They're now in their last year of seminary and have 150 Russian immigrants involved. The group takes on social justice issues and focuses on helping immigrants assimilate into a new culture. They still meet in the multicultural church's building, but intend to launch a stand-alone Russian immigrant congregation next year.

Talent spotters: In searching for potential church planters, it's best to find as many fishing pools as possible. Build relationships with key people who function as spotters of talent within organizations where leaders seem to emerge —it will save you time. You may ask some of the pastors you work with who are the mavericks in their congregations (the people always pressing for new things, never satisfied with the status quo, etc.). These people are often untapped leaders.

Christian educational institutions: Christian educational institutions may also be good sources of church planters, especially if church planting is part of their ministry training curriculum. Some organizations have been willing to help develop church planting curriculum and provide internships that serve as a doorway to accessing some of the graduates. Youth groups and college/career groups within churches also provide excellent places to find planters.

The harvest: Look also to the harvest. The harvest is the best place to find potential planters, yet sadly, it's often the last place we look. If an organization is working within a particular ministry focus group, who will be best equipped to reach that group? Those who are experienced in the culture—those who are a part of it and can reach out to others they know in the community. If no one fits that description, you'll need to start with others who are willing, but as soon as possible, begin raising leaders from within the harvest.

About three years into a church plant within a primarily Mormon community, a man named Peter began attending the church. He was on a journey. He'd been a faithful Mormon his whole life and was a spiritual overseer within the Mormon church. Peter had a true thirst for spirituality and as a Mormon was always seeking to go deeper. He began checking out Christian churches to learn more about them and how to undermine Christian teaching. When he heard a class on the fundamentals of the Christian faith advertised, he thought, "Perfect. I'll go to that, learn what they believe, then start converting Christians to Mormonism."

But what the class actually did was create a lot of questions in his mind. So Peter decided to go to a lot of different Christian churches to check on consistency because he'd been taught that Christian churches all believe something different and are confused about their own beliefs. As he was floating around to different Christian churches, Peter decided that the Mormon Church was not the answer to his spiritual thirst. Over the next five years, he went through a transitional process where he came to faith in Christ but still had Mormon teachings mixed together with Christianity. After all, he'd been a Mormon his whole life—that was the culture he knew.

After five years, Peter came on staff at a church as a director of outreach. He started helping the congregation become more effective at formulating their ministry so it communicated effectively to Mormon people. He had a vast network of relationships throughout the Mormon community so that, in any given service, between 30 and 50 curious Mormons were attending. Peter also created a video explaining what Christians believe using Mormon thought and terminology. It was a professional, top quality production, and the church would give a copy to anyone who came as a guest. Peter was a key leader in translating Christianity into the Mormon culture. He could reach the harvest because he had come out of the harvest himself.

Building relationships with potential church planters

The central role of relationship in attracting and mobilizing planters cannot be overstated. The sooner you can begin to cultivate authentic relationships with viable candidates, the better. In today's postmodern world, relationships are primary and cannot be based on structure or formality; there must be a strong personal element. With younger leaders, that relational element is especially crucial. Be sure to include strategy for developing sincere personal contact in any plans for recruitment.

As you begin building relationships, target certain people. Develop a prospect list and commit to a plan for working that prospect list. Sometimes potential leaders just need some encouragement. Having someone in a position of authority say, "Have you considered planting? I think you might be good at that," can bring about an increase in confidence and a willingness to rise to the challenge.

A denominational leader was interviewing candidates for existing pastoral openings. As he talked with one candidate, he felt compelled to ask him, "How would you feel about planting a church? We're looking for planters." The candidate didn't have to think long: "I'm resistant. Absolutely no way."

The denominational leader took it in stride. He assured the candidate they would continue to pursue an existing church opening, and added, "If you change your mind, let me know." The pastoral candidate went home and found himself bouncing around the house feeling excited. His wife noticed. She asked, "You want to plant a church, don't you?" Although he hadn't articulated his change of heart yet, his wife was right. They eventually decided to plant. Those responsible for recruitment shouldn't be afraid to broach the subject with potential planters, even if there's initial resistance. You never know!

Key people to help you find new planters:

- District/regional church multiplication team
- Pastors of healthy churches who have caught the vision for multiplication
- Leaders of educational institutions
- Small group leaders

Increasing the number of candidates

As you look toward increasing the number of planting candidates, keep in mind that mobilizing planters needs to be everybody's business. Recruitment is a team effort. Although certain team members will carry primary responsibility, everyone in the organization should have a vision for raising up planters and should keep their eyes open for leaders with potential. Shared responsibility for recruitment increases the number of potential contacts.

If an organization is just now beginning to be truly intentional about church planting, it is likely that in years past the numbers of church plants have been hit and miss. An intentional plan to plant multiplying churches, coupled with a clear recruitment strategy and vision, will almost certainly increase the number of church planting candidates each year.

Some groups successfully attract more potential leaders through high visibility events. A leadership or church growth seminar may attract a crowd that contains one or more potential church planters or other key team players. Church planting within a denomination tends to build momentum if it is given strong leadership. As a ground swell of commitment to church planting develops, the number of church planting candidates will increase. You can help this process by demystifying church planting and reminding your constituents that church planting is God's "preferred method" of harvest.

The more you can think creatively and come in behind what pastors are already doing, the better. A pastor was beginning an after school program in a poor community on the edge of town to work with girls on their self-esteem. The girls were beginning to ask her, "Can we worship together? Can we do praise? We have no church to go to." They didn't feel comfortable going into the more affluent neighborhood where the pastor's church was located even though it was only ten minutes away.

After talking with that pastor and hearing about what she was doing, a denominational leader asked her, "What if we hired you full time just to work that community with those girls and see what happens?" What they now have after three years is a congregation of 140. Seventy percent are under 17: it's children bringing children to church. The pastor has developed a trust level in that community, which is very hard to break through, and the denomination came in behind her.

The pastor is now forging a partnership with the local government. They are helping her secure land by putting pressure on some absentee landlords so the church can build a community center. The church would then own the community center as a separate nonprofit and the local government would run a medical clinic and a police department out of the center under a rental agreement.

Feeding church planting success stories like these into a group's communication system (both formal and informal) will also help ensure a growing number of candidates. Keeping the process visible and accessible will yield great dividends. Right after one church sent out three planters, a young man saw the parent church pastor and said, "Hey pastor, train me. I'll go." Although he had spoken lightly, he was serious, and the parent church pastor responded, "You're on my list anyway."

Short checklist

Use this checklist to lead your team through a planning process for attracting sufficient numbers of church planters to your district. This checklist is designed to help you, whether you are just beginning the process or seeking to improve it.

IDENTIFYING ROLES AND DETERMINING MOBILIZATION NEEDS

- Number of church planting projects and church planters required has been determined for the next 3-5 years.
- Additional church planters needed for church planting initiatives from parent churches have been determined.
- Names of solid church planters (commitment and proven ability) have been listed.
- Number of church planters still to be recruited has been determined.
- Means for recruitment of church planters has been listed.
- Other roles needed for the church multiplication process have been determined and methods for recruitment have been brainstormed.
- Ideas as to how we might prepare people currently serving in other roles for being church planters in the future have been listed.

ENHANCING DISTRICT EFFECTIVENESS

- Blockages to church planter recruitment in our denomination, vision, or process have been considered.
- Action plan to remove unnecessary blockages have been determined.
- Distinctive elements of our denomination, vision, or process that might be attractive to church planters have been identified.
- Major benefits we believe we offer to church planters have been identified.

- Strategy for improving our attractiveness has been prepared including who, what, when and a follow-up date for checking progress.

PROVIDING MATERIALS DURING RECRUITMENT

- Lists and description of the tools and materials we currently have that positively present the distinctive elements and benefits of planting churches within your ministry have been prepared.

- Each material/tool has been evaluated for its date and appeal.

- Material/tools needing updating have been listed with who will take responsibility for this and when they will have the materials updated.

- Material/tools have been listed which still need to be produced. Specify who will take responsibility for this and when they will have the materials produced.

BUILDING RELATIONSHIPS WITH POTENTIAL CHURCH PLANTERS

- The role and extent of prayer in our recruitment process has been evaluated and clarified.

- Intentional and comprehensive process for intercession to raise up workers has been determined.

- Current recruitment strategy has been clarified using chronological detail by citing what happens at each step.

Chapter Five

Developing church planters

Training with the end in mind

George Patterson planted churches and trained pastors in Honduras for over 20 years. When he first began developing church leaders, he followed the only model he knew: he opened classrooms out in villages to make pastoral training available to those who could not leave their crops, families, jobs, or animals to attend a residential Bible Institute. This method had worked well for denominations that already had churches and only needed to train their pastors. Yet for his purposes, the method was failing. Those he trained were unable to raise up their own churches and pastor them. Ultimately, he found that he could not multiply churches without leaders or leaders without churches. The two needed to be raised up together. When that started happening through on-the-job training, both churches and leaders began to multiply.

Leaders are raised up most effectively when teaching and experience are combined. And the best environment for that kind of hands-on training is the local church. Since different people learn in different ways, multiple training approaches are needed for optimal effectiveness. Classroom training alone will not suffice. Recognize that, at least to a degree, the kind of delivery system you choose preselects those who participate. A classroom-based approach will attract people who like structure, will repel people who don't like to read, and will feel irrelevant to people who are action-oriented doers.

My own bias is toward those training methods that are more life and ministry-oriented. I believe the more hands-on a training system is, the more likely it is to be fruitful. In a sense, learning how to plant churches is like learning how to swim. You can't teach swimming in a classroom. Think about how you learned to swim. Did you watch films on swimming? Read textbooks on the principles of buoyancy? Memorize the names of different types of strokes? No. You may have been given a few preliminary instructions, but you went into the pool, splashed around a little bit, and held onto the side. Then you practiced kicking, still holding onto the side. Then maybe you put your head under the water and blew bubbles, learning not to be afraid. It was a step-by-step process, but was primarily experiential.

It's the same with training church planters. Clarify the specific skills that are needed: what do they need to be able to do? Then go after experiences that will sharpen those skill sets. I was once talking to the dean of an academic program. I asked him, "After people graduate from this program, what can they do?" He told me later that question had kept him up at night for months. Most people have not thought through what outcomes they hope to accomplish.

As church multiplication movement leaders, we need to move toward a character and competency based training process—not just an academic one. We need to take seriously the mandate to raise up church planters. And we need to recognize that some of the people God wants to raise up to be planters are not yet Christians. Leadership development starts in the harvest.

Discovering Jesus' training paradigm

By expanding your horizons beyond trained, ready-to-go planters to include existing Christians and those in the harvest, you tap into vast new fields of potential. Yet since many of those candidates will be lacking traditional credentials, a strong development and training process is required.

How does that training take place? Too often people perceive training as something we send people away for. In many settings, formal training has become our default method. Promising young leaders go away to Bible College or seminary, then come back "prepared" for the ministry. Yet that's not how Jesus trained his disciples. Jesus used hands-on training—a kind of teaching that is paired with experience. I've often called it show-how training.

- I do, you watch
- I do, you help
- You do, I help
- You do, I watch
- You do, someone else watches

Not only did Jesus practice this method, but we also see it at work in successful church multiplication movements. Training is most powerful when combined with real life experience; people learn best when they have an immediate need for the information that is being taught. And the local church is the best context for this kind of hands-on learning.

That's not to say that formal training events should be avoided. There's a place for skills training, theological training, and regional or national level training events. Yet for helping people remember the lessons they're learning, nothing beats the local church. Coming face to face with real-life ministry situations has a way of making lessons stick. Let me tell you a story that demonstrates how Jesus trained his disciples through one of those real-life situations.

Jesus had taken three of his disciples—Peter, James, and John—up to the mountain for the transfiguration while the other nine stayed at the foot of the mountain. A father brought his demon-possessed son to the remaining disciples and asked if they would cast the demon out. By this time, I imagine the disciples had a rather successful winning streak going against these demons. They probably had cast out 25 or so in a row. They most likely approached the man's request with confidence, saying, "No problem." We'll take care of this. We've done lots of these before."

They commanded the demon: "In the name of Jesus, come out," but the demon threw the boy into a fit. Dust started flying up, all kinds of commotion was going on, and the casting-out just wasn't working the way it usually did. I can visualize the disciples huddling together to confer, sweat starting to form on their backs because the situation was getting a little tense. The commotion was such that a crowd has gathered around. The pressure was intensifying and they just couldn't seem to get the job done.

Just then—when things were almost out of control and they were about to give up—Jesus came down the mountain with Peter, James, and John. He entered the scene and asked, "What's going on?" The father broke through the crowd to explain. "I think it's my fault, sir. I took my boy to your disciples to cast out this demon. I really thought they could do it, but apparently they can't. I'm really sorry for all the mess and confusion I've caused." Jesus asked the man a couple of clarifying questions, then cast the demon out.

After the crowd had dispersed and the dust had settled, Jesus and his disciples were alone. Then they asked, "Jesus, why did it not come out for us?" Jesus answered, "That kind only comes out with prayer."

Now, why didn't Jesus cover that in Demonology 101? Maybe he did, but the disciples hadn't learned it. The reason they never learned it was because they had never needed that information before. Guess what they never forgot again? The next time they needed intense prayer to get a demon out, they knew it. People learn best when they sense a need. As much as possible, incorporate real-life experience into the way you train church planters. Initial training is often helpful and necessary to cover some basics, but ongoing training and coaching must continue throughout the planting process as questions and needs arise.

Recognizing this dynamic, many groups are forming experiential learning communities. These communities are groups of three or four people coming together for regular meetings, learning together as they minister. Most of the work is done outside of those meetings. This method can be adapted in various ways to meet planters' needs for ongoing training.

Good training produces lasting benefits:

"Do you not know that in a race all the runners run, but only one gets the prize? Run in such a way as to get the prize. Everyone who competes in the games goes into strict training. They do it to get a crown that will not last, but we do it to get a crown that will last forever." (I Corinthians 9:24-25)

Evaluating training needs and developing plans

To ensure a quality system for leadership development, current training systems need to be evaluated. Evaluation should be done on the basis of desired outcomes—are those who finish the training program clearly better equipped as church planters?

Educators often talk about "value-added" education. The basic process is below:

- Evaluate candidates before training to see what skill sets are needed

- Monitor along the way

- Evaluate again afterwards to see if all necessary competencies are present

- Recognize any gaps in the system

One of the strengths of value-added training is that it can be tailored to meet the specific needs of individuals. One very visionary, relational, creative church planter simply didn't understand the importance of details.

It wasn't until he completed his initial training and went out into the field that he really began to understand that if you miss the details, you can discourage your coworkers to the point that they won't want to work with you again, and the whole project becomes in danger of collapsing.

In the case of this planter, a system was in place to provide individually adapted follow-up training through personal coaching. The planter was given specific responsibilities and taught how to go through a checklist to follow projects through. His coach commented on the process: "When a person has potential, we'll provide initial training, get them involved in ministry, then continue to release them into more responsibility. That methods allows me to see where the planter is gifted and what areas still need work."

Training evaluation checklist:

- Those involved in evaluating the training process represent a wide spectrum of people and perspectives (trainers, trainees, neutral third parties)
- Post-event surveys and "exit interviews" for those completing a training regimen
- Evaluation results go to those who have the authority and ability to make needed changes
- Evaluation is translated into concrete plans for change

In considering potential changes to a program, be certain that each change improves the capacity to reach a desired, defined outcome. Any evaluation system that does not produce at least some modifications in the training process is a bit suspect. One organization found it had to alter its training to make it less detail oriented and give the planters more time for action planning. Just that minor change brought about significant improvement. That said; resist the need to continually alter training processes, materials, etc. simply for the sake of change. Such "tweaks" can frustrate those involved in overseeing and presenting the training.

Cultivating on-the-job training and coaching

- As discussed at the beginning of this chapter, experiential training is essential. Consider local church environments where you can provide on-the-job training and coaching for emerging church planters. What are the characteristics of a healthy environment for raising leaders? Some initial thoughts are listed below.

- Environments that produce leaders generally have multiple opportunities for leadership development (cell ministries, Life Transformation Groups, coaching with key leaders, etc.).

- An apprentice attitude: "We're here to develop you do what God has called you to do" vs. "You're here to help me out and do whatever I would like to have off my plate."

- Especially for emerging generations, leadership development environments must be highly relational, team-oriented, and involve a coaching component.

- Healthy environments place significant emphasis on excellence, yet give permission for leaders to fail in ministry attempts.

A seasoned planter recalls a time early in his ministry when he rented a high school gymnasium and big-screened the super bowl as an outreach event. He mailed out 30,000 flyers, organized a half-time party, and coordinated a kids' carnival for moms and kids who didn't like football. When the big event came, he found that the vast majority of those who came were already Christians. He also discovered that he'd brought in six different ethnic groups, most of whom spoke little English. After all the time and expense, very few people came back to the church the following week. Yet the planter learned from that experience and was encouraged by his coach and other team leaders to keep trying—better to try and fail and learn than not to try at all.

Anyone who examines different environments for raising up leaders will find that certain churches and ministries will be noticeably more fruitful in terms of producing leaders. Identifying and partnering with these churches or ministries can be a good first step toward creating multiple environments for on-the-job-training. Look at currently effective leadership development systems for reproducible philosophy and methods that can be transferred to other situations. And remember that other groups similar to yours are also asking these questions. Networking with others and linking with the larger body of Christ will create synergy.

Make the best use of whatever leadership training you've already got in place—improving the leadership production capacity of existing environments is always a wise first step. Yet the success of that kind of retooling will vary from group to group. Don't limit your long-term leadership development potential by relying too heavily on systems already in place—sometimes you may be better off creating new structures.

Implementing orientation and training processes

As you begin the process of developing leaders, begin with what you want them to look like. What knowledge, skills, and character traits will they possess? (Be sure not to confuse these essential elements with style or personality.) Starting with the desired outcomes will help you decide on the best training methods and processes. For instance, if you want relational planters, make the training process relational in style and build in relational components, such as leading groups and engaging in evangelism.

One of the most crucial qualities of a good training and developing program is making sure it's reproducible. The apostle Paul established a system of training that was reproducible, yet still high in quality. The original trainers pass down not only content and information, but the mandate to teach others: "And the things you have heard me say in the presence of many witnesses entrust to reliable men who will also be qualified to teach others" (2 Timothy 2:2). People often misinterpret this verse as talking strictly about discipleship, but remember the context: This was Paul talking to Timothy about pastors raising up other pastors. The way to start a church in the first century was by bringing people to Jesus and then congregational-izing them. Like every other aspect of church multiplication, the process and structure of training leaders needs to be built to reproduce.

An experienced pastor and coach tells the following story:

"A man and his wife came into one of our churches right out of Bible College and approached us about the possibility of planting a church. One of the first things we did was an initial assessment. It flagged some problem areas, but they were certain God was calling them to plant a church. Instead of saying no, I gave them a training alternative. I said, 'Based on the assessment results, we're not quite sure you're ready yet. We're not saying you're not called, just that you may not be ready at this point. What I'd like to do is give you an opportunity to get some more training and build your skill sets. If you develop the neces-sary skills, you'll have the opportunity to plant a church with us.'

"They agreed. We met for regular coaching appointments, and I gave him ministry assignments and responsibilities that I thought would enhance areas he needed to develop. One quality the assessment highlighted as needing improvement was 'building a cohesive church body'—a quality exemplified by developing groups as a foundation, quickly including newcomers into a network of relationships, monitor-ing morale, and using groups effectively.

"The man and his wife were not particularly relational people. By nature, neither was outgoing. When they first came to our church, they would leave immediately after the service instead of hanging around and connecting with people. Since we know how important relational connection is in planting a church, we knew we needed to improve this skill area. My intention was to deconstruct his paradigm of church being about services and programs and introduce a new paradigm of church being a community of people.

"I gave the man a challenge strategically targeted toward this growth area—and it came with a built-in incentive. I said, 'If you can start a small group, raise up apprentices, and multiply it a couple of times, then you can take all of those people with you as part of your core team to start a church in this area.'

"The man worked hard to strengthen his relational abilities, and multiplying the group was strategic in helping him develop those skills. When they left to plant a church—with four groups in tow—the change was marked. Phenomenal growth had taken place in their lives."

In this case, it's easy to see how training was not only tailored to meet individual needs, but also resulted in church multiplication. Coaching and training relationships for church planters need to be intentional, with clearly defined outcomes and expectations. The vital role of coaching in that process will be discussed more fully later in the book.

An intentional strategy for church planting, when coupled with effective, hands-on training, will increase the number of church planters being sent out. The increase should continue to grow as successful church plants arise and become a source of encouragement and learning. One key to continued multiplication is to have new plants start with the genetic code of multiplication already built in. As new leadership is developed, church multiplication will be the natural byproduct. Each new church should be launched with apprentice church planters who can be released to undertake another planting within the first three years of the new work, so vision for multiplication is built in from the very beginning. An intentional, reproducible training system will encourage churches to be continually looking for potential planters.

Increasing the number of churches raising leaders

To help more local churches become involved in raising up leaders for church planting, begin casting vision among the pastors. The best pastors to start with may not always be the most popular or those with the largest churches. Try starting with those who have healthy ministries and a genuine heart for the harvest.

Tips for working with pastors:

- Helping pastors see beyond their own parking lot is usually best accomplished in a venue away from their church. Inspirational retreats with other pastors are often a good setting.

- Demonstrate the value of "spiritual parenting"—both in raising new leaders and in launching new churches. Many such pastors will gain satisfaction and take appropriate pride in having such "spiritual children."

- Pastors are busy, so whatever training and coaching you offer them needs to be compact and readily accessible. Consider all the options: face-to-face, phone, internet, or electronic media.

Once some key pastors are on board, consider what kind of leaders you should be training. Ralph Moore, a seasoned veteran of church multiplication, suggests starting with servants: "If you train a rebel, all you end up with is a trained rebel."

A church multiplication movement leader had been overseeing the formation of a West Indian church in Chicago. The church had started at a grassroots level and was in need of a leader. The multiplication movement leader contacted a man he knew from out of state, who moved to Chicago solely for the purpose of being an apprentice. He worked with the multiplication movement leader for a year, slowly assuming more and more responsibility, and eventually he took on the role of pastor.

When asked why he thought the man would make a good apprentice, the multiplication movement leader said, "Here was a deacon, a faithful, mature man, who wanted to exercise his preaching and teaching gifts. Most churches wouldn't give him the chance to preach because he hadn't been to seminary. He lacked the formal theological training, but he definitely had the theological formation. With the right opportunity and hands-on training, I thought he'd do well. Plus he was from West Indies, so there was a good cultural fit as well.

"Yet the most important quality was that he was so humble and teachable. He moved, met new people, and did whatever had to be done. All I told him was that there was a lot of opportunity to be involved in ministry and church planting; I made no promise of a pastorate. Yet he came up as an apprentice and demonstrated a willingness to be developed with no timeline. He was prepared to stick it out no matter how long it took. All along I knew he was going to take over the leadership of the church."

Emerging leaders can often be challenged by being given a role that stretches them a bit. Good coaching will allow you to place people in roles that are just a little beyond them. Most people respond well to a challenge, especially those who are demonstrating leadership potential.

Ensuring that new churches retain the vision

One of the major challenges of a church multiplication movement is helping newly planted churches stay on track with the vision for church multiplication. As a long-time multiplication movement leader put it, "You're not successful when you have a daughter church—you're successful when you have a granddaughter church."

Churches committed to multiplication will have it in their "genetic code." In other words, the development of leaders for the purpose of multi-plication will be clearly present in vision and plans and their actions will be consistent with their statements about multiplication. Incorporating the idea of ongoing leadership farm systems into basic church planter training can help build a strong genetic code for the future.

Helping new churches build multiplication into their genetic code and keeping that vision alive is the responsibility of the church multiplication movement leader. That vision will need to be reinforced often because of the many potential distractions that develop during a church's birth and early development. Seek out practical, creative ways to keep multiplication fore-most in the minds of new churches. Some multiplication movements use a highly visible apprenticing system. Every new church plant begins with both a planter and an apprentice planter, who is expected to plant the next church. The system isn't just limited to planters either. The more roles that have apprentices in place, the more likely they are to multiply. Designating apprentices right from the beginning builds multiplication into the DNA in a way that is a visible reminder to all who are involved.

Developing a system-wide apprenticing process

Creating or maintaining a multiplication mindset can be bolstered by developing a system-wide apprenticing process. Apprenticing should not just be limited to planters. Extend the concept to every area of the church multiplication system—include coaches, trainers, group leaders, worship leaders... any area that will need to reproduce. The movement will break down if vital training cannot be passed on from one generation of leaders to the next.

All systems must be able to reproduce in a "fractal mode"—reproducing in all directions—not just in a tightly defined, linear way. As a need arises in one part of the system, the system itself should be able to produce the needed element. An organic, reproducing system will help keep the momentum for church multiplication going.

Systems like this generally require a good deal of adaptability. A group of German churches were working with three Hungarian planters who had demonstrated a lot of potential but lacked the financial means to attend many training conferences. In response, the churches designed an intensive, personalized incubator training just for them. It focused on areas where the planters would need additional help. Coming from the east, they hadn't had as much training in organizational and planning skills so the German churches walked them through how to plan the church year, how to design sermon series, and how to organize leadership development for church planting. They provided checklists, lots of materials, and personal training. Since the planters have returned to Hungary, they have multiplied over 31 churches.

As we train leaders, we must remember that a leader, by definition, has apprentices. Without this central concept, the church multiplication process will be limited to a linear progression—addition as opposed to multiplication—and may die out within a few generations as available personnel are used up. One way to ensure that leaders have apprentices is to make it a non-negotiable part of leadership expectations. An important note, however, is that having apprentices means giving them freedom and responsibility—and giving up your own control.

A multiplication movement leader who was overseeing the planting and developing of children's Bible clubs in an urban area tells the following story:

"A lot of our staff were asking the same questions, so we had a forum where they could help each other out by brainstorming solutions together. One major question they had was how to work through indigenous leaders rather than simply doing the ministry themselves. How could they train up new leaders and learn to work through others?

"Our staff were used to running the Bible clubs, controlling the quality, choosing the curriculum, inviting the people, etc. Now they're trying to switch to a paradigm where they say, "'We're going to train Juanita from the community to run the Bible club." And the way she does it might be a little less structured than the way we would do it. The kids might be bouncing off the walls more than we're comfortable with, the snacks might not be what we would provide. But we need to let that be and let them do the ministry, because they're going to be taking it over.'

"The staff are beginning to ask questions about ownership and responsibility. Whose ministry is it? How much of the training we provide is helping them become excellent vs. how much of my view of excellence is culturally biased? These are significant questions they could be asking as they seek to raise up leaders from the communities in which they work."

Leaders need to spend time thinking about what they do to raise up other leaders and whether those actions have a positive or a negative impact. Sometimes apostolic leaders successfully coach and release others without being aware of all that they do to facilitate that process. In those cases, it may be helpful to have a coach come alongside those apostolic leaders to help them analyze what they are doing—what works and what doesn't—so they can strengthen and streamline those areas that are working best.

Short checklist

Use the following checklist to evaluate the overall health and functionality of your church planter training system. You may find it wise to describe certain areas in addition to checking them off. Any areas that you cannot check off should be incorporated into your future planning exercises.

EVALUATING TRAINING NEEDS/DEVELOPING PLANS

- Criteria to evaluate incoming participants have been developed.
- Criteria to evaluate the training process (curriculum, teachers, mentors, etc.) have been developed and published.
- Criteria to evaluate the outgoing participants have been articulated and put into use.
- Regular times for evaluating our training process have been set.
- Who will be involved in the evaluation and who will receive the results has been determined.
- Procedures for making adjustments to our current program and persons responsible for doing so are in place.

CULTIVATING ON-THE-JOB TRAINING AND MENTORING

- Environments in which mentoring or training is already happening have been identified.
- Environments that could be re-purposed to include raising leaders have been identified and plans for restructuring them have been developed.
- New environments that raise up disciple-making leaders from the harvest have been created.
- Characteristics that make an environment effective for raising leaders have been identified and articulated.

IMPLEMENTING ORIENTATION AND TRAINING PROCESSES

- Simple, reproducible methods for developing leaders have been developed and deployed.
- Evangelism has been successfully integrated into our leadership development systems.
- The main limiting factor for multiplying training has been identified and strategies have been developed for overcoming it.
- Methods for mobilizing and training mentors are in place.
- The number of church planters being developed in our region is increasing.

INCREASING THE NUMBER OF CHURCHES RAISING LEADERS

- Pastors in our district with whom we can begin sharing the vision for raising up church planting leaders have been identified.
- A timeline describing who will contact these pastors and when they will do so has been created.
- Methods for helping pastors "see beyond the parking lot" and reach the lost through leadership development have been developed.
- Training opportunities for pastors interested in augmenting their leadership development are being provided.
- Coaching for pastors wanting to get training for leaders started in their churches is being supplied.
- Resources to assist local churches in training each level of leadership have been developed and disseminated.
- Roles and responsibilities in a church plant that can be delegated to emerging leaders for hands-on experience have been identified.

ENSURING THAT NEW CHURCHES RETAIN THE VISION

- Indicators that identify new churches showing a commitment to church multiplication have been articulated.
- Means for encouraging new churches to continue to produce leaders have been developed.

DEVELOPING A SYSTEM-WIDE APPRENTICING PROCESS

- Systems that need to be reproduced in order to maintain a church multiplication movement have been identified.
- Reproducibility has been maximized in our major systems.
- Things that we are doing that need to be reworked to make them more reproducible have been isolated and targeted for revision.
- Means for encouraging every leader to reproduce him/herself through apprenticing have been developed.
- Methods for increasing the effectiveness of apostolic pastors who mentor and release church planting leaders have been developed and deployed.

Chapter Six

Assessing church planters

Getting started with assessment

Assessing planter candidates is a solid investment in the future of a church multiplication movement. Taking the time and effort to choose the best candidates for leadership will make a difference—both now and for years to come. Put a reproducible assessment process in place now that can expand to meet the increasing need for more planters in the future.

A good assessment will benefit both the sending organization and the planter in many ways:

- Assessment helps good planters become better planters by revealing their areas of strengths and limitations. This information helps the planter build their team around what they have discovered about themselves.

- A clear selection process eliminates bias, blindness, and favoritism.

- Assessment protects the integrity and financial investment of the sponsoring church or agency. Planting a church can be expensive, and assessment helps groups make wise use of the resources God entrusts to them.

- A foundation is laid for a positive future relationship with the planting candidate. Assessment is an especially helpful tool for the coach assigned to the planter.

- Assessment helps the selection committee constructively redirect those likely to fail in a church-planting situation, thereby saving the candidate the pain and self-doubt that a failure brings. It can help protect the prospective planter's marriage, family, and other relationships from the damage associated with a failed church planting effort.

- Several denominations have recently banded together to organize a church planter assessment process. They help each other maintain the discipline of doing good, behavioral assessments and have designed a system to ensure quality and accountability. Just by investing in this one area they've already seen remarkable changes in their church multiplication efforts.

Establishing a system for assessing prospective church planters

One denomination recently completed a research study that found statistically significant links between planter assessment and church growth. Over the first four years of a new church plant, planters who had been assessed led churches that were an average of 20% larger than those of unassessed planters. One likely explanation is that assessment screened out people who shouldn't be planting. Although some may find the idea of formally assessing a church-planting candidate unsettling or unspiritual, up-front assessment is critical for successful church plants.

Planting New Churches in a Postmodern Age by Ed Stetzer. P. 79. *

Almost all church groups do some sort of assessment on prospective planters, at least in an informal sense. Most groups evaluate the character and doctrine of those they deploy. Yet a more formal assessment process broadens the scope of evaluation by addressing additional areas of consideration:

Strengths: Ask what are the strengths each candidate possesses and whether these are the right strengths for the planting assignment. Weaknesses may eliminate a person, but the effective leader starts by identifying strengths.

Necessary skills, competencies, and giftedness: Skills and competencies are best objectively assessed through a behavioral interview, which probes the candidate's proven behavior using appropriate criteria predetermined for the specific calling of church planting.

*For more detailed information on this study, see Edward J. Stetzer's 290 page study, The Impact of the Church Planting Process and Other Selected Factors on the Attendance of Southern Baptist Church Plants, Ph.D. Dissertation, The Southern Baptist Theological Seminary, 2003.

Character qualities: Character is naturally assessed through observation, over time, in a coaching relationship. Other steps that might be taken include gathering personal references, conducting interviews, and administering personality tests.

Emotional and marital stability: Leaders who finish well maintain healthy relationships with family and friends. Include family members of the potential planter in the interview process.

Theological understanding: Knowledge can be assessed through the traditional credentialing process (licensing/ordination exams) or through an informal process to help a potential candidate assess his/her biblical and theological understandings and growth areas.

Philosophy of ministry: A clear philosophy of ministry, which is formed out of a leader's experience, values, and unique gifts and calling, will help you assess a leader's compatibility with your organization and will increase their own effectiveness. Philosophy of ministry should be assessed not only by listening to the planter's statements of philosophy, but examining their past behavior to see if it falls in line with that stated belief system.

Think long-range regarding assessment. Ensure quality by taking some of the steps below:

- Build in regular evaluation of the assessment process so key areas can be improved.
- Assign someone the task of checking quality, being sure they are given specific criteria for good assessments.
- Think long term regarding ways to train an increasing number of assessors so the ministry capacity can be expanded.
- Try to train assessors who are located near the areas targeted for church planting.
- By deploying church planters who know how to raise up leaders from the harvest, you'll eventually have a supply of potential planters and assessors flowing from earlier church plants.
- Stay current with regard to assessment tools that are available; check online databases such as CoachNet (www.coachnet.org) regularly.
- For assessment to be legitimized in any group, senior leadership must actively support and promote its value.

- Those responsible for coordinating the assessment program should also be responsible for "championing" the assessment process.

- Assessment results must be kept confidential and should be reviewed only by those familiar with their purpose and use.

To demonstrate its support of the assessment process, one denomination hosts a "self-assessment weekend" where prospective church planters come to find out more about church planting with that denomination and assess themselves as possible planters. A denominational leader encouraged a young pastor just two years out of seminary to attend. The pastor expressed reservations; he didn't see himself as a planter. The denominational leader encouraged him to attend anyway—just to see. The pastor came away from that weekend with a new perspective. The only model he'd had in mind for church planting was a parachute drop, but after the self-assessment weekend, he looked at himself and said, "What I am really called to do is to start a satellite church out of an existing congregation—attracting a different segment of the population with a different style of worship, Bible study, and teaching."

Implementing behavioral interviewing

One of the most effective assessment methods is behavioral interviewing. Past behavior is the best indicator of future success. In order to effectively predict future behavior, selection interviews must focus on past behavior. Experience and vision are important but are not accurate predictors of future success. Research continues to demonstrate that consistent patterns of behavior in the past are the best predictors of future behavior. That's why a behavioral interview acts as the foundation of any strong assessment process.

Many lay people who are not directly called to church planting themselves can play an effective and essential role by serving as interviewers who can call out specific past behaviors of planter candidates. Most ministry candidates are so used to responding to questions with theory, ideas, and abstractions that they often don't bring actual behavioral examples to the table. Likewise, most interviewers don't generally ask for specifics, assuming that if a candidate says, for example, that evangelism is important, the candidate's life reflects that belief. The more assessors are able to bring out concrete examples of past behavior, the more useful data will be available for making well-informed decisions.

Since most planter candidates aren't used to communicating at this level of specificity, it sometimes takes a great deal of time and effort to get there. One planter remembers a lengthy interview where every time he went into theoretical explanations of his beliefs, the assessors nudged him gently back on track asking for specific examples of specific behavior. If they asked what level of contact he's had with non-Christians, he'd say, "Yes, I've had lot of contact with non Christians. I believe that's really important. If a planter can't relate to non-Christians, how will he be able to attract seekers instead of just transfer growth—" "Tell me about some of those interactions with non Christians." "Well, my wife and I invited some of our neighbors over for dinner and started to get to know them and their kids. It was good." "Tell me about that interaction over dinner. What did you talk about? What kinds of connections did you make?"

Most assessors find including the prospective planter's spouse helpful. As one planter put it, "I went into that meeting wanting to say all the right answers, the great answers that I thought the assessors wanted to hear. But a good assessor seeks the behavior, and having your spouse there is tremendous. Sometimes it's tempting to give a padded answer—not an untrue answer, just one that puts a bit more of a positive spin on things than is warranted—but you can't do that with your spouse there. I think my wife balanced my optimism with a more realistic perspective on some of the difficulties we've faced in our past ministry experiences."

At times, evaluating marital stability is part of the assessment process and assessors need to know what to look for. One assessor remembers a couple where the planter was the bolder of the two, but they were absolutely necessary to each other in terms of their gifts complementing one another. Even in the interview setting, the prospective planter's wife was freely sharing her concerns about this venture, while also sharing her faith that God was calling them to do this. Seeing the two of them interact and converse freely in the presence of others showed the assessor how confident they were in their relationship with each other, with the Lord, and with others. They spoke without animosity or tension, but with honesty.

No matter what the circumstances, assessors can still find creative, effective ways to examine past behavior. That same assessor remembers the first time he interviewed a candidate with no formal ministry experience: "Most of the man's examples came from his business experience and he was apologetic about it, but it was easy to see how leadership gifts could be used in a secular world just as effectively as in the spiritual world. He wasn't in any way diminished in his ability to plant a church because all of his experience came from the workplace. If anything, he was more equipped—he had so much life experience to relate to those who are searching for truth."

Mobilizing and training assessors

Since effective assessors must be able to ask probing questions that examine past behavior, and then be able to compile their findings in a concise and useable form, the importance of mobilizing and training good assessors is clear. Your assessment process will only be as good as your assessors.

As you mobilize people to fill that role, remember to look for good interviewers and listeners, not salesmen. Women often make discerning assessors. Avoid the "Barnabas" types, who want to encourage everyone. Important abilities include keeping matters confidential, not jumping to conclusions, guiding and probing without becoming directive, maintaining objectivity, and writing cogent, concise reports.

Assessors may be found in less than obvious places. Don't be afraid to look beyond your usual circles. There may be laypersons in your existing churches who are ideally suited (or even already trained) for selection inter- viewing. Making church planting a highly visible part of your organization may help you find and mobilize assessors from previously untapped sources. Enlisting a large number of assessors will make it easier for you to locate some who are nearby your target areas.

Many church groups compensate their assessors for their labor. Since this is a highly professional process, it is certainly fitting to have remunera- tion be a part of the reward for serving in this capacity. Check with other groups to see what they consider reasonable.

To have well-trained assessors, you'll need some qualified trainers. In identifying trainers, you should think not only about initial training but also ongoing training for additional assessors as they become necessary. Consider offering "brush up" training to current assessors as your program develops. Planning for training needs should take into account attrition of assessors as well as an increased number of candidates when multiplica- tion starts to happen.

Some good sources of training for assessors include the pioneering work of Dr. Charles Ridley, the "Training for Selection Interviewing" material available from ChurchSmart Resources, and denominations and organiza- tions that have assessor training in place. A user-friendly assessor's guide and clear guidelines for assessment make the training of assessors easier and more effective.

Assessors should be evaluated on the basis of how well they:

- Understand the behavioral assessment process and philosophy
- Conduct effective interviews (by remaining objective and asking effective questions)
- Evaluate the results of their interviews (objective, clear, based on given criteria)
- Report the results (thorough, concise, understandable and well-written)

Once some initial training has been completed, try teaming newly trained assessors with more seasoned veterans during interviews. This type of pairing will hasten and enhance learning. Additional coaching can also be done during the initial training sessions during which trainees do mock assessments (usually partial interviews) under the watchful eye of a coach.

New assessor training processes are not likely to be fully effective from the start. Plan to evaluate, modify, and retrain as needed. Encourage regular feedback from those who will be receiving and using the assessment reports. Don't leave evaluation and improvement to chance—decide now how assessors will be evaluated and who will be responsible for doing it.

Ensuring a quality assessment process

Prework: Denominations vary widely in what they require of planter candidates before the assessment interview. Some possible activities include assessments in other areas (marital, emotional, etc.), pre-assessment interviews, working through "The Church Planter's Toolkit" (or at least part of it), submission of applications, and statements about doctrine and experience. The goal of this initial process will weed out those not sufficiently committed or qualified and will alert the candidate to the rigors of what lies ahead.

Interviews: Once candidates have completed these initial requirements, interviews should be conducted in a warm but neutral environment close to the beginning of the selection process. We strongly recommend having at least two assessors present for each interview—it's helpful to have a second set of eyes.

Communication: Even if literature has been given to candidates earlier in the process, go over the planter position description verbally to clarify expectations. Provide opportunities for candidates to ask questions, inform them of the next steps in the process, and conduct a second round of interviews with promising candidates. Clear and open communication is a must.

Assessment results: Results of the overall assessment process should be provided in a timely manner to the appropriate decision-makers. Face-to-face delivery is best, as the person presenting the results should be capable of answering questions about the assessment. Because of the sensitive nature of the material and the potential for misunderstanding, avoid merely mailing the results.

Criteria: The use of uniform and fair criteria for measurement and evaluation is crucial to a healthy selection process. Consider looking for standardized tools as launching points for your discussions of criteria. Candidates need to be sure that what they are being measured by is demonstrably important to success in church planting. The use of instruments such as the "Church Planter's Profile" and other standardized, objective tools will help ensure consistency and reliability in the use and application of criteria. Groups can certainly develop their own instruments or modify existing ones (if legally allowed to do so), but retaining objective and uniform standards is easier when learning from what others have done.

Evaluating the process: One of the best ways to build a strong assessment process is by evaluating your current one. List out the processes or steps that are currently involved, formally or informally. Then evaluate the effectiveness of your current selection process by computing the percentage of successful church plants. Experience and research show a positive correlation between thorough, intentional assessment and successful church plants. What percentage of your church plants are viable churches after three years? After five years?

Discerning errors: The only way to improve your current selection process is to discern selection errors made in the past. The list of common selection errors in this section may stimulate thinking. Once you have determined your group's weaknesses in the past, you can use that information to build a selection process that gives objective and accurate assessment in the areas of character, theology, and competence that are essential to healthy church plants.

Top 5 assessment errors

- Not looking at enough candidates
  (The goal should be at least three candidates per planter.)
- Inadequate position description
- Lack of clear criteria for selection
- Incomplete investigation procedures
- Ineffective interviewing process

Equipping candidates to submit proposals

Although research and planning cannot replace the call of God on the heart of the church planter, neither does the call of God replace the need for careful and thoughtful preparation. Requiring proposals ensures that some advance preparation and thinking has been done. Yet planters often need help creating acceptable proposals. The more specific an organization is regarding expectations and criteria, the more likely they are to receive satisfactory submissions.

Good proposals generally include:

- The planter's core values and vision statement
- Evidence of demographic research
- A written philosophy of ministry
- A preliminary strategy for reaching the target group and achieving initial goals
- A proposed budget
- A clear statement of call and a rationale for the church planter's desire to plant a church at this time, in this location
- Team assignments, in the case of team effort church plants
- A timeline
- A ministry flow chart
- A plan for enlisting ongoing, faithful prayer support

Evaluating proposals

- Once you have established the categories proposals should include, decide who will evaluate them and with what criteria. It's also wise to establish in advance who else may receive a copy of each planter's proposal. Coaches should certainly have access to them, but others may benefit by the information as well. Consider especially core team members, intercessors, and financial supporters.

- Begin by ascertaining the depth and accuracy of the demographic research; cooperative efforts among denominations can cut down duplication in this area.

- The vision should demonstrate realistic goals. Vision should be large enough to require faith and attract people, but should not go beyond faith to presumption or delusion. When evaluating vision, the church planter's own gifting and experience need to be taken into consideration.

- Evaluating a proposed budget should be done on the basis of cold, hard economic realities. Is the church planter going to an economically depressed area with high unemployment? That should be taken into account. Is the church planter planning to be a "tentmaker"? If so, what income will his/her job skills generate in that environment? Is the planter counting on donor support? If so, there should be firm evidence of that support.

- When evaluating strategy, watch for gaps in the plan. A good strategy will clearly build on itself and have an orderly flow, yet be flexible enough to allow for the unexpected. Strategy should also align itself with core values and vision and take into account the amount of energy required to accomplish it. Finally, is the strategy realistic? Can it be accomplished by the people and resources allocated to it in light of God's expected enablement? If the strategy requires a miracle at every point, it is neither biblical nor realistic. Even a cursory look at the Apostle Paul's strategy shows a blend of human effort and ability plus supernatural supply and direction.

Once a church planter has been assessed and accepted, they should be commissioned and supported in a way that encourages them and affirms their call to church multiplication. Depending on the individual organization, commissioning church planters will have various "tribal factors" related to it, but should always be done in such a way as to legitimize and make official the planter's role in the eyes of the group.

Yet remember that working with individual planters doesn't end with assessment. The relationship continues through coaching, planting, and finally church parenting. These are not just planters you are assessing—they are the future leaders of the entire movement. Seek the Lord's wisdom and guidance in helping you choose wisely.

Short checklist

Use the following checklist to evaluate the overall health and functionality of your current assessment and commissioning systems. You may find it wise to describe certain areas in addition to checking them off. Any areas that you cannot check off should be incorporated into your future planning exercises.

WE HAVE A SYSTEM ESTABLISHED FOR ASSESSING CHURCH PLANTERS THAT OBJECTIVELY ASSESSES:

- Necessary skills and competencies
- Christian character
- Emotional and marital stability
- Theological understanding and skill
- Philosophy of ministry

OUR ASSESSMENT SYSTEM HAS...

- Effective procedures for recruiting assessors.
- Effective procedures for training assessors (initially and continually).
- Effective procedures for supervising assessors so that quality control is happening.
- Functioning procedures for ensuring the timely submission of reports to the proper individuals.
- Functioning procedure for timely review of the assessment(s) and a timely response to the candidate.
- Functioning procedures for one-on-one reporting to the candidate of the results of the assessment(s) and any decision related to their candidacy.

WE HAVE IN PLACE A PROCESS THAT HELPS CANDIDATES TO SUBMIT WELL-PREPARED CHURCH PLANTING PROPOSALS THAT DESCRIBE...

- Their target group
- Their values
- Their vision
- Their initial strategy and team assignments (if applicable)
- Their projected budget
- Any other requirements placed upon them by our denomination or group

THE PROCESS FOR PROPOSAL DEVELOPMENT INCLUDES...

- Training and coaching in the preparation of the proposal.
- Clear instructions on where and how to submit the proposal.
- A timely review and response procedure for submitted proposals.

Chapter 7

Coaching church planters

Introduction

From the outside, coaching can be one of the least visible components of a church multiplication movement. Yet behind the scenes, it provides that essential personal element that brings life and direction to key leaders in those movements. Without individual leaders being empowered and guided through coaching, continued multiplication will not happen. No matter how competent the leaders are, they'll still get bogged down if they try to go it alone. We need others to help us along the way—that's part of God's design.

The pastor of an established church was planting another church on the side that was rather non-traditional. "The Family Church" targeted kids, and services were held in the late afternoon. The plant wasn't going well and the planter wasn't finding much support from his community. Almost ready to give up, he stumbled upon a coaching group. Within that framework he found the encouragement and support he needed. His vision and energy were renewed, and the plant survived and continues to grow.

If coaching is so important, organizations need to ensure that their capacity to coach planters expands along with the number of planters they are developing. Think long-range. As with every dimension of church multiplication, we need to focus not just on coaching, but on increasing coaching capacity. The ultimate goal is to create a system that develops and raises up more coaches to supply the future need for them as the entire movement grows and reproduces. Although at the beginning you may need to recruit experienced coaches from outside your movement, eventually new coaches will be raised up from the ranks of those who are currently being coached. Yet to create that kind of successful, multiplying coaching movement, certain pieces will need to be in place. You'll have to develop a comprehensive coaching plan—and that begins with mobilizing some initial coaches.

Mobilizing coaches for church planters

Most coaches, especially if they have other full-time responsibilities, can handle only one or two active coaching assignments effectively. Therefore, most groups will probably need to raise up quite a few coaches to oversee their planters.

So what qualities are important in potential coaches? Good coaches are people who can be trusted, people who are perceived as caring. Look for those who naturally empower others and are helpful to them, those who can listen well and ask good questions, and those who don't feel they have to tell others what to do. Ask yourself if this is a person who can resist the temptation to tell his or her own stories. For the issue isn't how the coach did it—the issue is what God is calling this new planter to do.

Look for people who:

- Have good character
- Share vision and values
- Are loyal
- Are respected by other leaders
- Empower others for ministry
- Have a teachable spirit
- Have the ability to lead a ministry
- Have the ability to multiply ministry
- Have the ability to listen and care
- Have the ability to strategize and train
- Have the ability to challenge and confront

Avoid people who:

- Have a problem with pride
- Need to lead rather than coach
- Need to control others
- Are over committed to other ministries

Source: Ogne, Steve and Nebel, Tom. *Empowering Leaders Through Coaching* (St. Charles, IL, ChurchSmart Resources, 1996)

Noticing potential coaches: There are many people around who, with the right training, would make excellent coaches. You just need to know what qualities to start looking for. Try to open your eyes to people who may have previously gone unnoticed. Coaches are often less visible than other more traditional, up-front leaders. Sometimes the qualities of a good coach become apparent at unexpected times. A denominational leader remembers introducing a church planter to another man at a conference. The two of them began talking, and when the denominational leader came back half an hour later, the conversation was still going. The man seemed to understand the planter's perspective and was interested in helping him ask the right questions instead of just answering questions. The denominational leader thought to himself, "Now that's a coach."

Introducing people to coaching: When you recognize a good potential coach, contact them personally to talk over their possible involvement in coaching. Be sure to provide clear information on qualifications and responsibilities, including the time investment required. Cast a vision for church multiplication, and the role coaching plays in it. Before committing, potential coaches must understand the goal of church multiplication and how they fit into the larger picture. Candidates who are truly qualified will prayerfully consider the invitation.

Planning for coaching: What will you do if and when some of those potential coaches accept? A training plan should already be in place by the time invitations are made. Initial training should be thorough and put a number of resources into the hands of your coaches, including coaching guides and refresher material. Several groups include the first year of membership in CoachNet as part of their training package. Many coach candidates also choose to participate in church planter training as apprentice coaches.

Training for coaching: Effective coach training is designed to be transferable. The person who oversees the setting up of training for coaches should be prepared to develop a strategy for ongoing training and support, not just a one-time event. Coach training should also include an apprenticeship—experience with supervision is just as essential as the initial information-based training.

Matching coaches and planters: Next a system must be in place for matching coaches with planters. The best systems not only link planters and coaches together early in the process, but also reproduce themselves. One such coaching system is currently operating in Australia. Before anyone is trained to be a coach, they must have experienced three months of coaching themselves. As they are coached, their coach both models and explains the coaching process. During this time, the potential coaches read *Coaching 101* and find two people who they will coach. Only after taking those steps do they attend coach training—a two-day intensive during which they work through the *Coaching 101 Handbook* together. For the next six months, the new coaches continue to receive coaching while they coach the two people they've recruited. At that point, the whole process reproduces itself and the people who have been receiving coaching become coaches themselves. This system is now its third cycle, with an 85 to 90% success rate for coach retention and reproduction.

Evaluating coaching: Confidential feedback from both coaches and planters will help determine if the match between coach and church planter is a good one. Strong matches result in supportive, challenging relationships. A planter tells the following story about his relationship with his coach:

> "I was getting to the level in my church plant where it felt like the next logical step was to get out of church planting mode and get into church mode—where you have more programs, more meetings, more maintenance. I found myself spending more time doing pastoral counseling, which is not my gifting. I'd been trained that that's what pastors do and I wasn't fitting into the mold. I saw myself as a planter—raising people up and equipping the saints to do the work of the ministry—but I couldn't see myself as a pastor. I didn't know how to handle it, and felt like I was falling flat on my face. So I went to my coach and told him about it. He said, 'Who told you you have to do that?' 'Well, I thought that was the next logical step,' I said. His response was, "Why? Why not take the energy and creativity of a church planter into the church? To give it up doesn't make any sense."

That coach gave his planter a needed sense of perspective. He knew his planter's gifts and could speak directly into his context, encouraging him to continue in what God had called him to do.

Training and supporting your coaches

To ensure coaching quality and continuity in a multiplication movement, ongoing development opportunities are essential. Offering regular, follow-up training communicates to coaches that they will continue to grow even after their initial training. In fact, those subsequent training opportunities often prove to be even more profitable since coaches will bring real-life questions to the table.

Ongoing training and support implies a long-term goal: the fully trained coach who can go on to raise up other coaches. Thanks to the recent completion of a qualitative research project on coaching competencies, we now have a better picture of what that fully trained coach looks like. The nine most important competencies discovered are listed below:

Foundational competencies

- Relies on a strong spiritual foundation
- Pursues self-knowledge, self-development, and improvement
- Communicates effectively through listening, asking questions, and giving feedback

Relational competencies

- Establishes a relational bond with the person being coached
- Supports an ongoing coaching relationship through encouragement, challenges, accountability, provision for needs, and clarification of focus and direction
- Recontracts or brings closure to the coaching relationship at the appropriate time

Strategic competencies

- Assesses problems or situations accurately by gathering and evaluating data
- Helps people set goals and create plans for achieving those goals
- Evaluates progress toward goals and makes needed adjustments

These competencies can help drive the process as a whole. After coaches have been on the job for a while, they can get an assessment, identify areas where they need to improve, and then design a personalized plan for their development. That type of overall process makes training more focused.

Awareness of the coaching process, along with some basic coaching skills and competencies can be further fleshed out through resources like *Coaching 101* and *Developing Coaching Excellence*. Groups of coaches can read these books together and work through the practice exercises as a team. Well-selected coaches will almost certainly want to hone their coaching skills. Many groups find it advisable to make two tiers of training available: one that is required of everyone and one that is optional—either more advanced training or a refresher course.

Empowerment. Without empowerment, real coaching cannot happen, for the process of coaching is not about the coach—it's about the person being coached. Finding and living God's agenda will look different on every person. Coaches aid that process of discovery, but they don't direct it. Coaching is not about telling others what to do—it's about helping them discover it for themselves. The goal of coaching is not to make carbon copies of oneself, but to empower others to live out God's unique design for their life. Coaches who learn basic coaching skills will begin empowering others, and coaches who empower others will be making use of basic coaching skills.

George Patterson, missionary and multiplication movement leader in Honduras, initially served as the primary church planter early in his ministry. Whenever he went out to start a new church, he took a Honduran national with him to help. Yet Patterson found that those nationals did not begin seeing themselves as planters but continued to view themselves as assistants. They were not being fully empowered.

To help people begin shifting their thinking, Patterson called together key workers and leaders from established congregations and they studied the Great Commission. Then, taking a large blank piece of cardboard, he roughed out a map of the area and had the leaders fill in all known villages and existing churches. Patterson then asked them how they were going to reach the other villages and establish new churches. At first the national leaders felt overwhelmed because there were too many villages to reach. But slowly they began to take it one step at a time, looking for villages that were close to them geographically or in which they had connections. The new churches that could be established this way would then go on to join the effort in reaching other villages.

Patterson also empowered those leaders by phasing out methods that were not reproducible in their culture, such as using airplanes or cars to travel from village to village. In coaching appointments, he had the leader he was coaching sit behind the desk instead of himself. He empowered local leaders to perform functions that often required ordination, such as serving communion. By methods like these, Patterson helped the leaders under him see themselves as planters and pastors, and—by empowering them to take the lead and make their own decisions—he promoted church multiplication.

Patterson, George & Scoggins, Richard. *Church Multiplication Guide: Helping Churches to Reproduce Locally and Abroad*

Creating coaching environments

Coaching needs to be incorporated systemically so it's infused at every level of ministry. Coaching isn't just for planters—we need to create overall environments that are conducive to coaching.

Consider different groups who could benefit from supportive relationships. Every one of these groups is essential for the emergence of healthy new churches:

- Spouses
- Core team members
- Parent church pastors
- Coaches
- Denominational leaders
- Pre-Christians
- New Christians

Consider also the different types of coaching that might work well for different groups. Fortunately, the coaching system is versatile enough to be delivered in multiple ways:

- One-on-one coaching
- Peer coaching (peer coaching often works best in groups of three)
- Group coaching

New Church Incubators (NCI) provide a good example of how good, supportive coaching environments can be created. Planting teams from across an area gather monthly with their coaches in the NCI for support, ongoing skill training, and implementation planning. In some cases, pastors of established area churches are involved. Within this environment, coaches can work with planters and planters can provide feedback and ideas to each other as well. NCIs will be discussed in more depth in chapter 9 on networks.*

Ongoing training for coaches: Ongoing training and mutual support for coaches will help them continue to grow. Try to create a community of coaches. The internet and the phone provide means of connection regardless of geographical distances, yet encourage face-to-face contact whenever possible. Peer relationships, whether formal or informal, will help coaches realize they aren't in it alone, that others face the same challenges they do. Coaches need these types of supportive networks and relationships to thrive.

Online coaching: Online coaching can often increase coaching capacity as well. Just recently I was showing someone how to use CoachNet's online coaching function, and he said, "Oh, I could use this with so-and-so who I'm coaching." Remind your coaches that instead of trying to be supercoaches, they should keep it simple. By using easy, reproducible methods that others can duplicate, more coaching happens and more new coaches get raised up.

Coach accountability: Some type of regular reporting is generally necessary to ensure consistently high quality coaching. Having people in place to coach your coaches will also help provide accountability. The Pygmalion Principle says that leaders tend to rise to the level of your expectation: this goes not only for planters but for coaches as well. Yet remember the impact of positive reinforcement. Benefits, recognition and encouragement will provide a necessary balance to reporting requirements and will help keep your coaches motivated.

One coach alone can't do everything. Networks allow not just one coach, but a whole family of support for a planter. One young planter discusses his experience with the support community coaching provided for him: "I'd previously had an unsuccessful

*The original NCI work has been revised and expanded by Robert E. Logan in consultation with Steven L. Ogne. Please see the reference information in the bibliography.)

planting experience with no coach. Then the second time around I had a coach. It was a night and day difference. I have found a family around me in my denomination that continually supports me, resourcing me and communicating with me on a regular basis. It's been awesome to have this core of people around me to help me. If I've got a question and my coach doesn't know the answer, he can direct me to someone who does. Before I always felt like I was at the top of the ship and beyond that there was no support. With coaching I found a new strata—there was this whole support network above me."

Developing coaching movements

Building a coaching system that grows and expands with a church multiplication movement means that new coaches will continually need to be raised up—and one of the best places to look for those new coaches is among the planters who have benefited from coaching. Not every church planter makes a good coach, but some of them would be excellent. Because of their experiential learning process, those who have successfully started a church can be extremely helpful to others who are just starting out.

Once their plant is mature enough to demonstrate their basic competence, planters can be considered for a coaching role. This approach makes the process reproducible, increasing long-term coaching capacity. You'll be able to continue developing and raising up new coaches from within instead of having to recruit more and more from ever-diminishing outside pools.

Identify these emerging coaches by using the same grid you did for your first coaches. Look for coaching qualities and listen to feedback—current coaches can often readily identify other potential coaches. In fact, coaches who are currently doing a good job may turn out to be one of the best sources for raising up more coaches: they know what is required and probably have additional networks of relationships to tap into. Ask your coaches to be on the lookout for other potential coaches, and enlist them to help develop the new coaches they find.

The long-term health and viability of your church multiplication movement requires an ever-expanding pool of qualified coaches. Developing second and third generation coaches is vital to keeping a coaching movement on track. Some key areas to focus on include:

Selection of qualified coaches: Choose people who have coaching competencies, available time, and a heart for planters.

Training coaches deeply: Coaching as both a skill and an art is essential. Don't settle for just basic level training.

Assessing coaches: A formal assessment system using behavioral interviews, coaching competencies, and rating norms can help coaches design personal growth plans.

Reproducibility: Each coach should have an apprentice—most often a recent planter. This structure will facilitate generational multiplication within the coaching movement.

Maintaining focus in the midst of trying to develop all of this can be difficult. There are a number of challenges to initiating and sustaining a coaching movement. Each situation will be unique, but common problem areas include developing new coaches, coaching "dropouts," accountability for coaches, quality control, time management for coaches, and coach vs. teacher paradigm problems. Although there isn't time here to address all the possible concerns, many resources exist to help leaders think through solutions for their particular challenges. A few of the better ones are listed in the appendix.

Whatever challenges you face, be sure to celebrate the significant milestones as you develop your coaching movement. Celebrating together will help generate and sustain momentum for your coaching movement, and will provide added visibility for church multiplication.

Short checklist

You can use the following checklist to evaluate the overall health and functionality of your current coaching movement. You may find it wise to describe certain areas in addition to checking them off. Any areas that you cannot check off should be incorporated into your future planning exercises.

COACHING MOVEMENT BASICS

- Sufficient number of coaches for church planters has been deployed.
- Sufficient number of coaches has been made available for projected church plants next year.
- Characteristics and proven abilities we look for in our coaches are clearly defined and published.
- Recruiting material for potential coaches is available.
- Clear instructions as to how interested persons can proceed are developed and published.

- Initial training, with adequate resources, for new coaches is scheduled regularly.
- Procedures for matching coaches with planters are in place.
- Feedback loops to determine whether the match is a good fit are in place.

ONGOING TRAINING AND SUPPORT FOR COACHES

- Ongoing training to expand our coaches' skill base has been developed and deployed.
- Definitions of which ongoing training is optional and which is required have been disseminated.
- Opportunities that allow coaches to share experience and insights have been provided (see also networks point below).
- A coach of coaches is in place and functioning.

RAISING UP NEW COACHES

- A process to identify church planters who will make good coaches is in place.
- Guidelines that help us determine at which point in their church plant we will invite them into a coaching role have been developed.
- Current coaches are being encouraged to look for potential coaches among those they coach and communicate this to us.
- Procedure to ensure that new coaches are themselves adequately mentored is in place.

INCREASING SUPPORTIVE RELATIONSHIPS

- A system to ensure the quality and consistency of coaching relationships is in place and working well.
- A reporting system for coaches with clear direction as to what is expected, how often it is expected and to whom reports are to be submitted is in place.
- A system for ensuring that recognition and benefits are passed along to those who perform well has been developed and deployed.
- Coaching networks with facilitators appointed who have clearly defined roles are in place and functioning well.

FURTHER DEVELOPMENT OF OUR COACHING MOVEMENT

- Milestones in the building of our coaching movement are being regularly celebrated.

- Primary challenges in our situation to improving our coaching movement have been identified.

- The challenges which are most strategic have been targeted for overcoming with plans laid for doing so.

Chapter 8

Parenting new churches

Cultivating vision for churches planting churches

Early reinforcement of a multiplication vision is essential. Without active vision casting, the arduous task of planting a church tends to diminish zeal for planting another. All social groups by nature tend to gravitate inward unless intentional intervention offsets this tendency. As you seek to cultivate vision for churches planting churches in your region, ask yourself what caught your interest and generated your commitment to church planting. A parent church pastor reflects on his own experience:

> "The reason I had the confidence to take risks in church planting was because of an experience I had early in my ministry when I was an associate pastor. Our church was running about 500 people on an average Sunday. We had raised up two planters and sent them out at the same time. I remember the Sunday we sent both these planters out with 50 people each to places within 10 miles of the parent church. If you do that math, you would think that the following Sunday there'd be 400 people in the parent church and 50 each in the new churches. That was true. But two months later we were stunned to find 700 people in the parent church."

That experience helped that pastor take risks for church planting, and stories like these can encourage others to take risks for the kingdom as well. Personal testimonials generally go a long way toward cultivating a vision for church planting.

Consider what other strategies will work to reach others in your district or region. If your churches typically respond well to Bible-based challenges, how will you present such challenges? For instance, more and more churches are adopting the position that planting new churches is more important than building projects—they are committed to planting before building. This vision is one that could be cast well through an appeal to scripture.

Another good strategy for communicating vision is to anticipate objections and respond to them before they are raised. Some obvious and common objections that you need to anticipate relate to costs (personnel and funds) and inward focus ("We can't even supply workers for our church, etc."). Both of these objections can be addressed from the biblical principle of sowing and reaping: "Give and it shall be given to you."

Increasing parent church health

As mentioned in the first part of this book, studies have shown that churches that plant churches are, on the average, healthier than those who don't. In most cases, church multiplication efforts actually serve to increase the health of mother churches.

That said, church health is a legitimate concern. Churches should be aware of their own strengths and weaknesses as they enter into the church multiplication process. Taking the Natural Church Development (NCD) survey is one of the best, most accurate ways to make this determination. It's a sophisticated tool designed to determine the health of a local church.

NCD has isolated eight quality characteristics essential for healthy, growing churches:

- Empowering Leadership
- Gift-oriented Ministry
- Passionate Spirituality
- Functional Structures
- Inspiring Worship Services
- Holistic Small Groups
- Need-oriented Evangelism
- Loving Relationships

Churches can use the NCD survey and implementation process to improve their health. The healthier parent churches are, the healthier the plants they produce will be. Combining church multiplication efforts and NCD church health improvement strategies will create a synergy in which each side sharpens and improves the other.

Mobilizing potential parent church pastors

A crucial step in any church multiplication movement is getting poten-tial parent church pastors on board. You'll need to find pastors who have the potential to plant and go actively recruit them, creating a process to identify, contact, and gain commitment from potential parent church pastors. They will then also need to be equipped and supported as they work to develop congregational commitment. The key concept in mobilizing parent church pastors is intentionality.

Identify: In most cases, you will probably know the pastors in your district or region well enough to know which ones are likely to respond positively to a vision for church planting. If not, discuss the matter with someone who knows them. Examine current productivity, potential, and teachability.

Contact: Once you have a list of potential parent church pastors, set some dates for contacting them. If initial contact needs to be deferred until some materials are developed so you are more prepared for those meetings, chart a timeline showing when the materials will be ready and when pastors will be contacted.

Gain Commitment: Pastors may get defensive when challenged to plant other churches. Resistance is often a natural first response. Deal with that resistance by first listening to fears and excuses. Dealing effectively with personal blockages will empower the change process, for personal change needs to precede corporate change. It won't take too many contacts with pastors to discover common patterns in terms of pastoral fears and objections, and those observations will help you address the issues in future contacts. In some cases, the values and models held by pastors may be real hindrances to a church planting vision. Anticipating these paradigm issues before making contact will help you shift them to more biblical values. As you talk with potential parent church pastors, think long-term. The question is not only how to get pastors on board initially but how to keep them on board. Lay out the vision for church multiplication as clearly as possible at the beginning.

A denomination in Germany has a vision for wanting all of their churches to be church planting churches. They adopted a strug-gling church and helped them through a church split. The church survived and began to grow and become healthier. Yet a year later when that newly adopted church heard at the next national

conference that the identity of the movement was church multiplication, they seemed quite surprised. "What is all this about
church planting?" they asked. "What do you mean that in order to
be healthy we have to have daughter churches?"

The denominational leaders learned from that experience. They
recognized that selective hearing can be one of the biggest
obstacles in working with potential parent churches. People hear
those things that will help them with their immediate needs, and
they tend not to register strongly those things they do not immediately recognize.

Equip: Once parent church pastors are on board with the church
multiplication vision, equip them well. Offer them guidelines and/or
training on vision casting, leading through change, the church planting process, etc. Recognize that they will need help finding ways to
cultivate congregational commitment. They'll need to identify key lay
leaders and opinion leaders (people who may not be official leaders
but who nevertheless have a strong influence over the congregation),
then learn to target "early adopters"—those who are first to embrace
change or fresh vision.

Support: In addition to equipping must come peer support. Create
Parent Church Networks (PCNs). These are special coaching groups
that provide a supportive environment for pastors of churches involved
in or interested in sending out daughter congregations. They offer relational support, peer coaching, and training in the planting process
from the parent church perspective. PCNs will be discussed in more
depth in the next chapter. Brainstorm additional ways you can keep
parent church pastors communicating with one another. Consider
district/regional conferences, CoachNet online, special small groups
at denominational gatherings, and other ideas. The support parent
church pastors receive from peer interaction will be substantial.

Increasing the number of parent churches

Building multiplication into the genetic code of new churches ensures
that more and more churches will be planted, and that those churches will
go on to parent other churches. If new churches get off to a good strong
start—with apprentice planters and a vision for continued multiplication—
they'll be prepared to parent well and you'll soon see an exponential rise in
the number of new churches.

With existing churches, more work may be involved. What are the prevailing views on church planting? How successful have past planting efforts been? How do the parent churches involved feel about those experiences? In certain cases, some damage control may be needed.

Remind parent churches that situations they view as failures may not necessarily be so. New daughter churches are supposed to be different from their parent churches, and that's okay. One mother church had been strongly focused on direct evangelism, yet its daughter church went the route of social justice, community activism, and helping people in need. The church has reached a lot of people, and its style of ministry reflects the hearts, gifts, and creativity of the planters.

Existing churches may need to do some initial work in the vision casting area as well. What would increasing involvement in church planting look like for them? Ask them to put some time into considering where they've been, where they are now, and where they would like to be in three years. Their responses will provide considerable data regarding the kind of planning work they need to do in order to become a parent church.

Short checklist

Use the following checklist to evaluate your plans to help churches parent other churches in your church multiplication movement. You will find the checklist more helpful if in addition to checking off certain areas, you respond in detail as needed. Any areas that you cannot check off should be incorporated into your future planning exercises.

HELPING NEW CHURCHES PLANT CHURCHES

- Ways to keep the vision of church planting alive in church plants have been considered.
- Plan for engaging church plants in planting more churches has been developed.

CULTIVATING VISION FOR CHURCHES PLANTING CHURCHES

- Key points to raise in sharing the vision with churches in our district have been clarified.
- Reasons for why we think they will be attracted to this vision have been considered.
- Objections they might raise, and how we will respond to them have been explored.

MOBILIZING POTENTIAL PARENT CHURCH PASTORS

- Specific pastors/churches that we believe would respond to a challenge to plant more churches have been identified.
- Contact plans have been devised.
- Plans on how to get them on board with the vision have been developed.
- Coaching assistance has been offered.
- A Parent Church Network has been planned with dates and location.

VALUES FOR PARENT CHURCH PASTORS

- Possible excuses and fears of pastors have been identified.
- Underlying values that hinder or enhance church planting have been identified.
- Ways to help pastors/churches shift to values that enhance church planting have been considered.

DEVELOPING CONGREGATIONAL COMMITMENT

- Ways to support the pastor in cultivating congregational commitment have been considered.
- Key people in the congregation who will need to be committed to planting a new church in order for a congregation to move forward have been identified.

INCREASING THE NUMBER OF PARENT CHURCHES

- Number of churches involved in church planting 5 years ago has been compared to the number of churches involved in church planting now.
- The percent of increase in churches' involvement has been prayerfully projected for the next 3 years.

Chapter 9

Developing multiplying networks

The need for networks

For church multiplication movements to thrive, people need to be in relationship with one another—communicating, exchanging ideas, and challenging one another. Planters need to have regular contact with other planters and coaches with other coaches. Providing networks for all groups involved in the multiplication effort will strengthen the movement's overall cohesiveness. Essential groups requiring networks include:

- Planters
- Coaches
- Parent church pastors

Establishing and maintaining these networks is essential to the effectiveness and functionality of a church multiplication movement. If the individual pieces don't work, the overall system won't work.

Next, consider what other groups involved in the multiplication movement might benefit from participating in a network of like-minded people. Brainstorm the kinds of networks that may need to be launched within the next few years. Not all special needs may be identified at the outset of a church multiplication movement, and the need for others may arise along the way, but take some time now to try to anticipate networks for people not yet mentioned. Some possibilities area listed below; fill in any other groups that come to mind.

- District leaders
- Regional leaders
- Trainers
- Spouses
- Intercessors

Networks often spring up in response to needs. Consider the examples below:

A leader was trying to help churches that were making the transition from a traditional style of church to a more cell-based approach. Because that change can be difficult, he saw the need to create a network to help churches walk together through the process. The result was Cell Transition Network. The change process often takes churches longer than they expect and they hit bumps along the way, but many are succeeding, in part due to the support this network is providing.

"My denomination wanted to send the husband and wife out as a team," explained one planter, "but they didn't have any support network for the spouses. The coaching group provided was just for me. My wife asked me, 'If we're really supposed to be in this together, what's there for me?'" Soon after this conversation, this planter's wife met the wife of a prominent church multiplication movement leader and sent her a series of questions via email. The multiplication leader's wife forwarded the questions to some other planters' spouses she knew, and together they built an informal online network of church planting spouses. "If you want a team, support both spouses," advised the planter. "Denominations need to get out of the 'two-for-the-price-of-one' paradigm. Many of them have networks for planters, parent church pastors, denominational leaders, coaches—and nothing for the women. Women are more involved in ministry that they ever have been."

In another case, a church multiplication movement leader began to see the need for a network that would promote cross-cultural understanding between churches. Diversity ran high in his region and church leaders often had difficulty understanding and appreciating the differences between their churches. The multiplication leader highlighted both the need and the benefits of such a network: "There's more that can be done to encourage a new level of cultural sophistication between evangelicals of difference—especially economic and racial differences. Many church multiplication efforts tend to be homogeneous. By working together we can accomplish much more, especially in terms of reaching new people groups."

Networks for different groups will necessarily look and function differently. Planter networks may need to facilitate frequent contact, while parent

church pastor networks may not need to meet as often. Networks for planting spouses may be more relationally support-based in nature, while coach
networks may focus more on accountability and ongoing training. The
success of a given network depends on whether it accurately discerns and
meets the needs of the group it serves—and that will vary from group to
group and movement to movement.

Notice that I've titled this chapter *developing multiplying networks*. My
use of the adjective multiplying is intentional. Networks not only support
church multiplication movements, they are an organic, intrinsic part of them.
They are designed to multiply along with the rest of the movement. Planter
networks should multiply to create more planter networks. Parent church
pastor networks should multiply to create more parent church pastor
networks.

Ultimately, denominations can even multiply to create more denominations and organizations to create more organizations. Out of Wesley's
Methodist movement came the Nazarene Church, the Free Methodist
Church, the Wesleyan Methodist Church, the Holiness movement, the
Pentecostal movement, and the Salvation Army. All were profoundly influenced by Wesley and have their organizational roots in Methodism. The rise
of Methodism also strengthened the Anglican Church, from which it came,
by challenging it and encouraging the birth of Anglican evangelicalism. The
multiplying nature of churches shows itself at every level, from individual
discipleship to the creation of new movements. Networks are one of those
crucial, multiplying components.

Establishing resourcing and training systems

Networks will form the primary relational and resourcing component
within a church multiplication movement, so consider what is needed to
build them and maintain their health.

Facilitators: Facilitators are one primary need. These people will need
to have demonstrated some gifting in facilitation and have a heart for
church planting. They will also need to be willing to take on the responsibilities and time commitments appropriate to the type of network
they will be coordinating. Some may be able to facilitate more than
one network, especially if those networks are not as time-intensive.
Work to identify the right people for these roles and supply the appropriate level of training, accountability, and support.

Resources: Next, consider other necessary resources. These will vary
from network to network, but frequently include meeting places,

training materials, etc. Networks that meet face-to-face less frequently may also benefit by online communication networks such as CoachNet.

Once network needs have been determined and facilitators have been brought on board, training will need to be provided for those facilitators.

Orientation: An initial orientation ensures that facilitators have a working knowledge of the church multiplication system and how all the various pieces fit together. For example, a planter network facilitator will need to know what training/information the planters within their network have been exposed to, and what commitments and expectations exist.

Initial training: After orientation has been completed, some preliminary training should be offered to facilitators. What this training looks like will depend on the network type. Facilitating an online network requires different skills than getting together with people face-to-face—and the training offered should reflect that difference.

Follow-up training: Ideally, ongoing and follow-up training should be driven at least in part by facilitator feedback and should focus on enhancing facilitator skills.

Facilitator support: Support systems are absolutely essential for your facilitators. Who will coach them? How will they network with others? Contact needs to be kept personal. Face-to-face support is best, with regular telephone contact coming in second.

Look to the future as you plan for network leaders. Consider unforeseen attrition and lay the groundwork for raising up facilitators from existing networks to ensure that multiplication continues. Just as you plan to raise leaders from the harvest in your church plants, you should plan to raise new network leaders from the existing networks. The apprenticing model can be incorporated into the fabric of the whole plan by asking current facilitators to be watching for and training apprentices. Today's network members are tomorrow's network leaders.

Multiplying networks for new churches

One of the most critical networks for any church multiplication movement is the network for planters. Although they are known by many different names, the type of planter network I'm most familiar with is the New Church Incubators (NCI). With NCIs, a group of planters and their coaches meet on a monthly basis to provide supportive, peer-coaching relationships. These meetings often take the form of ongoing skill training, trouble-shooting, and implementation planning. In some cases, pastors of established area churches are involved as well. NCIs create good, safe environments to bounce ideas off one another and give and receive feedback.

Answering the questions in this section can help you develop a plan for starting and multiplying NCIs—getting them out of the "great idea" stage and into functionality. Placing answers to the questions below on a timeline, with the "who" and "what" filled in for each stage will produce a workable plan for starting NCIs.

- How many NCIs do we need in our region?
- Where do we have three or more plants in reasonable proximity?
- Who are the possible participants?
- When and how will we recruit participants?
- When and where will the meetings take place?
- How and when will we involve key leaders and spouses?
- Who is prepared to lead the next NCI?
- What quality control will we use to ensure that NCIs are effective?
- Who will guide us through the process?

"The information exchange with other area planters can be really valuable," says one planter who met with an interdenominational NCI group to pray, encourage each other, and discuss ideas and strategies. "We used to bring in Christian bands for a public open air concert. One established church in town was predominantly funding it and the rest of us kicked in. One of the planters in my group said his church stopped funding it and I asked why. He told me that the vast majority of those attending the concert were already Christians. It was good to know that because that wasn't my understanding of what we were supposed to be doing—we wanted to use the concert as a platform for evangelism. If we're going to spend our money, we want to spend it wisely."

That same planter had also recently advertised his newly launched church in a coupon book that was mailed to 15,000 homes. It included nice color invitations and the other planters in his group wanted to know how that strategy had worked out. "Don't do it," he cautioned them. "It doesn't work. For several thousand dollars we had two people visit our church." Networks of area planters not only provide a forum for encouragement and discussion, but can also help planters avoid mistakes others have already made.

Strategic multiplication movement leaders will seek to plant three to five churches in close proximity, making it easier to facilitate NCI clusters. If this arrangement is not possible, consider linking your planting teams up with other groups who are planting in the same area or with existing area pastors. A planter working in a rural area of Texas utilized this approach. "My church planter training program told me that the first thing to do is to find the community of local pastors and join it. I did that and was so impressed by the support I received. We got together on a weekly basis to pray. One pastor donated a phone system and office furniture. Two of the congregations that were not part of my denomination and were not even charismatic decided to support our plant financially. They told me, 'We are under-churched and need more church plants in this area. We are more than happy to have you.'" When no other plants are in the area and the only support is provided by existing churches, planters should take advantage of online NCI support so they still some contact with others who are currently planting.

Also be aware of cultural issues within NCI networks. Just because plants may be close geographically does not necessarily mean they will be close culturally. If an NCI has planters from more than one cultural group, there may be issues that go beyond just having a common language. In many cases, the varying perspectives of these groups will mean they have more to offer, yet they also may require more work on the part of participants. Below is a partial list of cultural issues that may become problematic in NCIs or other networks.

- Time orientation —event orientation
- Either/or thinking —holistic thinking
- Crisis orientation —non-crisis orientation
- Task orientation —person orientation
- Status focus —achievement focus
- Concealment of vulnerability —willingness to expose vulnerability
- Each culture will act on these cultural value continuums in a different way. When someone from a time-oriented culture enters an event-oriented culture, adjustments in thinking and action will need to be made in order to relate effectively.

Source: Lingenfelter, Sherwood and Mayers, Marvin. *Ministering Cross-Culturally: An Incarnational Model for Personal Relationships*

If your organization currently has very little in the way of networks, a planter network is the one to start with.

Church planter networks are one of the most important networks to have in place to facilitate a church multiplication movement. Planters are often the people with the highest motivation to participate in a network and the ones who are most likely to recognize their need for such an environment. Investing in creating healthy support networks for planters will pay for itself many times over as new churches are born.

Building networks for parent churches

Like planters, parent church pastors will need support networks as well. Six Free Methodist pastors formed a parent church network (PCN), and committed to each planting a daughter church within 18 to 24 months. After a couple of months, the pastors of the two largest churches dropped out. (Larger churches often have more difficulty multiplying themselves.) The four remaining churches planted five new churches in the next 12 months. One church had twins—an English speaking church and a Spanish speaking church. Now these churches were not large—the smallest was only 45 people—but without the parent church network, it's likely that only one church would have been planted. One pastor had the vision and drive to do it alone, but the network provided the accountability, support, and focus to help the other parent church pastors follow through. It's similar to having an exercise partner—if you have someone to go running with each morning, you're much more likely to do it.

Building PCNs will require many of the same steps as building planter networks:

- Mobilizing facilitators
- Mobilizing coaches
- Launching networks
- Multiplying networks

The same questions in the last section can be applied to planning for PCNs as well. However, remember that coaches and facilitators for PCNs will need to be different from those for NCIs—they will need different experiences and perspectives and will need to be able to gain the respect of the pastors who will become a part of the PCN.

As with planter networks, it may be reasonable and helpful to consider networking with other groups in areas where your group doesn't have enough parent churches to form its own PCN. The disadvantage of linking with other groups is that, unless cooperation between the groups is extremely high, it usually does not facilitate multiplication as well. However, as the number of churches planting churches increases, the percentage of PCNs should increase accordingly.

Whatever the specific arrangements, plant the seeds early for involvement in parent church networking. An experienced area pastor was coaching a new planter in his area. He asked about some specific needs in the plant and cut the planter a check on the spot to cover those needs temporarily. As the pastor handed the planter the check, he said, "This isn't just about us giving to you. This is so that when you get your plant off the ground you can give to other ministries too." He encouraged the planter to become a parent church pastor as soon as possible.

Creating networks for coaches

As discussed in chapter six, coaches play an essential role in guiding and directing church multiplication movements. Supporting coaches helps ensure the strength of the movement. Networks for coaches allow them to get together to strengthen their skills, connect with like-minded people, and continue to grow in vision and maturity.

One example of a coaching support network is LEAD teams. Not all coaching will look like the LEAD team model—different ministry contexts will call for different options—but it may help create a picture of what coaching can look like. LEAD teams began when leaders of TeAMerica, the church planting and mobilization agency of the Baptist General Conference, recognized the lack of connection as a significant risk factor in church planting and renewal of existing churches. He noticed that the failure rate of new church plants went up when few other supportive churches are nearby, when the planter has no natural support group, and when the number of potential contacts in the area is low. In an effort to minimize those risk factors, he launched a new approach to coaching called LEAD teams.

Eight to ten leaders, usually established church pastors and planters, form a LEAD team. LEAD stands for learning, encouraging, achieving, and dreaming. They get together for a 24 hour period once every two months to learn something, build relationships and have fun, hold each other accountable for the goal of seeing one church planted each year, and share vision for church multiplication and renewal.

The combined power of mission and relationship is considerable. The people on LEAD teams are not necessarily all coaches—anyone involved in ministry and interested in church multiplication and renewal is welcome. Yet everyone has something to contribute to the planting project. Maybe one member recruits a planter, another coaches, another builds intercession teams, another contributes key core team members, and another assists with fund raising. Together they get the job done. The key is valuing both church multiplication and church renewal as two important features of the same movement. The kind of community support that develops for the planter and the project dramatically increases the chance of success. With LEAD teams in place, the survival rate of church plants has gone from 70% to 90%. One LEAD team in Washington D.C. plants not just one church every year, but three or four.

Having a coaching structure like LEAD teams in place makes the life of multiplication movement leaders easier because it increases owner-ship. Planters are no longer alone because they now get welcomed into a team and find a natural network of support. Many of these teams have been actively praying that God would bring them a planter. One LEAD team just had a planting couple approved through assessment and are eagerly awaiting their arrival. Although most of the LEAD team members haven't even met the couple yet, they are looking forward to that first meeting like parents look forward to adopting a baby. The paperwork has all been filled out and approved and they are anticipat-ing the big day of arrival.

How much different that is than having a multiplication movement leader come to area pastors and try to get them on board. "Hey, we have this new planter coming in. Could you get behind it? Could you coach him? Could you help him out?" Instead there is an ownership that comes from something eagerly awaited and prayed for. The burden for church multiplication is shared. Pastors who used to want to hold onto their youth pastors and associate pastors are suddenly willing to release them to planting efforts. And—like every other element of a church multiplication movement—LEAD teams are repro-ducible and designed to multiply, making the job of a multiplication movement leader even easier. Today's planters become tomorrow's pastors and coaches.

Other coach networks will take different approaches, but a multiplication movement that does not support its coaches soon finds itself lacking them. Coaches need to be able to come together to learn, to problem-solve, to give and receive encouragement, and to sharpen the vision God has given them for church multiplication.

Extensive networking is a vital part of the church multiplication process. The synergy that is developed cannot be duplicated by other means. Networks serve to increase the vision and the relationships necessary for church multiplication movements.

Short checklist

Use the following checklist to help you develop multiplying networks in your church multiplication movement. You will find the checklist more helpful if in addition to checking off certain areas, you respond in detail as needed. Any areas that you cannot check off should be incorporated into your future planning exercises.

ESTABLISHING RESOURCING SYSTEMS

- Networks needed for coaches have been identified.
- Networks needed for church planters have been identified.
- Networks needed for parent church pastors have been identified.
- Networks needed for special needs have been identified.
- Basic resources we will need to ensure effective networks (e.g. computers, on-line access, meeting locations etc.) have been acquired.
- Personnel and time commitment needed to organize these networks have been considered.

SUPPLYING NETWORK LEADERS' TRAINING

- Names of potential facilitators of networks for new churches, parent churches and special needs have been collected.
- When, where and how we will introduce potential facilitators to the facilitator role has been planned.

- The training facilitators will need before they can facilitate a network has been developed.
- Support systems for facilitators/coaches have been devised.
- Contingency plans for facilitators that aren't working out or who need to drop out for some reason have been developed.

RAISING UP LEADERSHIP FOR NEW NETWORKS

- Plan for multiplication of facilitators has been developed.
- Participants in current networks have been considered as possible future facilitators.

MULTIPLYING COACHING NETWORKS FOR NEW CHURCHES

- Contracts have been completed and material has been received.
- Facilitators/Coaches have been identified and trained.
- Possible participants have been identified and contacted.
- Participants have been recruited and matched with coaches.
- Venues and dates have been established for each network.
- Plans for multiplying networks for new churches have been developed.
- Quality control to ensure effectiveness has been established.

INCREASING COACHING NETWORKS FOR PARENT CHURCHES

- Contracts have been completed and material has been received.
- Facilitators/Coaches have been identified and trained.
- Possible participants have been identified and contacted.
- Participants have been recruited and matched with coaches.
- Venues and dates have been established for each network.
- Plans for multiplying networks for parent churches have been developed.
- Quality controls to ensure effectiveness have been established.

DEVELOPING COACHING NETWORKS FOR SPECIALIZED NEEDS

- Coaching networks for specialized need have been identified.
- Facilitators/Coaches have been identified and trained.
- Possible participants have been identified and contacted.

- Participants have been recruited and matched with coaches.
- Venues and dates have been established for each network.
- Plans for multiplying networks for parent churches have been developed.
- Quality controls to ensure effectiveness have been established.

Chapter Ten

Funding a church planting movement

Developing financial support

Financial support is an essential part of church multiplication. To get a sense of where you are and what is needed, consider both immediately available sources of support and potential sources of support.

Available: First begin to generate support for a church multiplication movement by tapping into funding sources that are currently available and accessible. Those funds can be incorporated into your planning immediately so you will know how much more support will need to be developed. Work to discover not only how much funding is available, but also how easy it is to disburse those funds and how flexible your organization's spending policies are. Funds that are available but locked into a rigid appropriation procedure are obviously not as useful as funds that can be quickly and readily disbursed. If your denomination or group has a rigid funding process, a good starting point may be to work with those who can make changes to loosen things up in terms of funding for church planting. That said, having some guidelines in place for the appropriate distribution of funds is also necessary. What factors do you believe are important to tie to funding? Spell these out in a written document. Be sure to include the amounts available for various programs and personnel, requirements in terms of fruitfulness, a policy of regular review, a reporting procedure for the accountability of those receiving the funds, and responsible parties for overseeing disbursements.

Potential: After tapping the funding sources immediately available, you'll then need to move on to developing other potential sources of support. Since the goal is to develop a church multiplication movement, you'll undoubtedly need to develop a plan for tapping into other sources of support for church planting well beyond those currently available. Each denomination or group has different sources available to it as well as different protocols for raising funds. Brainstorm as a team regarding this need, then develop a plan that attempts to project realistic expectations in terms of increased funding that will be available over the next two to three years. Constructing a timeline for that period showing the who, what, and when of how funds will be developed and deployed will also be helpful for ensuring faithful follow through.

Closing down ineffective programs

Ineffective programs can be terminated to release funds for church planting. Almost every organization has some programs that are truly ineffective, but eliminating them may be a delicate business. Making a case for their termination will be easier if you develop clear and reasonable guidelines by which effectiveness can be determined.

One key factor should relate to how various programs fulfill the mission of the organization. Christian groups are often burdened down with programs that have no clear connection to the stated mission of the group. Often these programs once had clear purpose and connection, but have long since shifted that purpose.

Church planting became a stated priority for one denomination, so they formed a team that had church planting as its mandate. However, others within the denomination believed it was important to revitalize or re-plant smaller struggling churches. The church planting team was designated to oversee both projects. Because the leaders of the denomination were regularly confronted by the smaller struggling churches, more and more resources went toward revitalizing these churches. After a few years, most of the original team that had a heart for church planting had moved on and the new members were asking for more and more resources and producing almost no results. Unfortunately, some programs may be "too sacred" to eliminate all together, but they could conceivably be made more efficient. Increasing the efficiency of current programs is another good way to release funds for better projects.

Another important part of the elimination of ineffective programs is the clear and persuasive presentation of how much better it is to use the funds for church multiplication. If you can make a stronger case for funding than other programs can, you will be more likely to win your case.

One of the most powerful but difficult means of eliminating ineffective programs is to convince those involved in the ineffective program that God has a better plan for them and for the resources allotted to them. Sometimes those involved in such programs are aware of their ineffectiveness and are longing for change. Approaching them with a bridge to building more effective ministry may bear much fruit. In some cases, staffing roles need to be realigned to make the best use of everyone's giftedness.

One denomination made a certain position half-time by cutting several unnecessary tasks and used the money to devote more resources to leadership development.

In most organizations you will not only need to begin the process of eliminating ineffective programs but also monitoring the entire procedure. Check back to see that programs really are terminated, and develop a process to trace the funds that are released to make sure that they arrive in the church planting budget area.

Stopping subsidies for unfruitful plants

It's not only ineffective programs that need pruning, but also unfruitful church plants. To do this, you'll need to define what you mean by unfruitful, develop clear guidelines concerning fruitfulness and funding, and create a redemptive process for church planters who have their funds terminated.

Defining "unfruitful" is admittedly a tough assignment, but teams do need to work through this issue. What will a successful church plant look like at six months, at twelve months, etc.? Keep in mind that some exceptions to the rule will always exist. Some mission fields are indeed "harder" than others. For that reason, it's critical that more than one person decide delicate matters such as termination of funding. A well-constructed team increases the likelihood that all factors are being considered.

The clearer you are in defining your expectations for church planters, the less likely you are to encounter painful confrontations about terminating support. Being able to look back at a document where expectations regarding fruitfulness are spelled out will help a great deal when it's time to discuss things with a struggling planter. Develop clear documents of agreement. Checking with other groups to see what they are using may be helpful. Remember also that any document relating to financial support should take the form of a signed agreement. It's much easier to discuss these matters with a signed agreement in hand than it is with only a subjective sort of understanding. It's probably also wise to include in the document some type of appeal or review process for the church planter to pursue. The process need not be cumbersome or complex—it can be as simple as an appeal to a denominational executive or a process of communicating with the planter's coach. The planter will be more likely to feel heard if there is some type of appeal process in place.

Developing a clear agreement about fruitfulness in advance can prevent long term, indefinite funding of failing plants, as many have learned the hard way.

One denomination empowered and funded a planting couple without any written agreement. The couple was well connected, so the typical requirements were waived with an attitude of, "We know you. You don't need to go through all this red tape." No strong accountability structure was in place. No planting proposal with objectives and goals was submitted. No assessment was done until after the couple was already appointed.

At that point, the couple went through an assessment process. Both the husband and wife were from rural, blue-collar communities. They had been appointed to serve in an upscale, white-collar suburban community. Most of the families living there had attended prestigious universities and worked in the high-tech field. In addition to the potential cultural problems, the planters were also missing certain critical skill sets. When the assessment team finished, they thought, "Oh no, this doesn't look good." But the couple had already been appointed, so the couple's coach tried to do what he could, working with them and helping them develop.

Yet the fact remained that the planting couple simply lacked the gifts and skill sets necessary to plant successfully in this context. Their core group consisted of a handful of elderly people, and they weren't held accountable for bearing fruit in accordance with a proposal. Finally, after a year and a half, the plant collapsed and the couple admitted they couldn't do it. Not only was the planting attempt unsuccessful and financially draining for the denomination, it was also unnecessarily painful for the planters.

Setting clear guidelines for fruitfulness in plants also serves to clarify vision and mission.

A declining church with an aging congregation made a decision for church planting. They said, "We're dying. We're a small group at this point. We want to sell our assets and help the denomination start a new faith community." The people were mostly in their 60's and 70's, with almost no one under 50. They said there needed to be a new way and a new day, and they wanted to be a part of something new that would reach their own children.

The denominational leaders overseeing that church thought the people had already done the preliminary work on vision, so they went out and found a pastor they believed matched that vision. The congregation sold all their assets and prepared for a new venture. But as soon as the new pastor arrived, they immediately wanted to have traditional worship services, complete with hymns and organ, and do things the way they'd always done them. The fruitfulness was simply not there.

The denomination recognized the new initiative wasn't going anywhere, and had to call a halt to it within nine months. The congregants were good people, but they just couldn't make the necessary cultural shift. Ending was painful for them, but they had begun to realize that this other style wasn't what they had signed on for, and that was probably why they weren't reaching their own children. The denomination redirected assets and assigned the pastor to a church that could parent more effectively.

Spelling out clear, agreed upon guidelines for fruitfulness at the beginning, and tying those expectations to funding can help avoid painful situations for everyone involved: planters, denominational leaders, and laypeople.

Creating a redemptive process for planters who don't succeed

Planting is a difficult venture and many good candidates don't succeed. A failed plant can bring a great deal of self-doubt and discouragement. "Those who start and fail go through sometimes years of self-condemnation and feelings of failure," explains one planter who saw the churches of several fellow new church incubator members fail. "Sometimes the biggest struggle is the last several months of a church plant that you know is falling apart. It's humiliating and you feel you have missed God." Planters deserve support during this difficult time. Put a redemptive process in place to lessen the strain for planters who have their funds terminated.

Obviously, the termination of financial support comes at the end of a process of trying to work with a struggling church planter and his or her team. Although relational support has been given along the way, don't leave it to chance during this last critical stage. It can be devastating for a church planter to feel "dropped" relationally due to a failed planting effort. As much as possible, involve the planter's coach in the decision-making process. Coaches are often in a good position to offer ongoing input when funds are cut off. In some cases the decision to cut funding may not mean the end of the church plant, of course, but in the majority of situations it will. You therefore need to be sure that you have redemptive and redirective systems in place for the church planters and their teams. They need both encouragement and new directions for their energy.

The following story is told by a parent church pastor:

"We invested $100,000 in a church plant in a very wealthy area. Paul, the planter, did all the right things: he was assessed, went to planter boot camp, and got a good coach. We tried to do it all correctly, but the plant struggled and struggled.

"Part of Paul's strategy was asking the question, 'What is it going to take to reach the hearts of these really wealthy people?' The Bible says where your heart is there is your treasure also. He thought that if he addressed the good they could do with their wealth, he might have a chance of touching their hearts. We designed an initial bridge building process, with one of the goals being finding ways to get these people to invest in ministries. Many area residents were in the medical field, so Paul started taking leaders in the community on medical missions trips. He created exciting medical missions initiatives by partnering with missionaries on the field. He'd give a brief presentation inviting people to go and take five or six of them. None were Christians and all invested heavily in Paul's medical missions ministry.

"In one case they went to partner with a single woman missionary in Central America who lived in a third world setting alongside the people she was trying to reach. The doctors and medical administrators were just blown away. They had never seen anything like this firsthand before. They started to open up and talked about spiritual things on the plane on the way back. Paul became their spiritual mentor.

"At that point, he launched the church. Yet even with significant financial backing from us, the plant wasn't able to create a worship environment that attracted these people. People's spiritual interests had been aroused by the missions trips and the missionaries they had met while there. They wanted to investigate Christianity further, so a lot of them went to a very strong, well-established evangelical Episcopalian church in town. When they decided to go to church, that's where they felt comfortable. We helped that church grow by leaps and bounds.

"While the plant continued to flounder, Paul created a separate nonprofit organization. Over the last three years, it has generated millions of dollars for medical missions. Paul invited me to attend one of the fund raising events that they had—a wine tasting in one of the homes in a private, gated community. I had to be picked up in a limo and brought to the house. Everyone there was a multimillionaire. Paul talked for five minutes about the new project they had coming up and invited people to give. He raised $500,000 with a five-minute presentation.

"The plant itself never really got off the ground. It fizzled. Paul had been so determined to plant a church that he was actually depressed. He was so focused on that particular goal that it was really a hit for him emotionally that the church plant didn't survive. He felt like he was a failure. We had to spend some time talking with him and helping him realize that something else had come out of his efforts. I remember saying, 'Paul, you may not have planted a church but you haven't failed here. The kingdom of God has been furthered.' He eventually moved on from that disappointment and is now full time at the nonprofit he founded."

Encouraging new churches to contribute

Build support for church multiplication into the genetic code of new churches. Even very recently planted churches can give something. It may not be a substantial amount, but the very act of giving will be incorporated into the DNA of the new church. If churches don't get in the habit of giving early, they sometimes don't get in the habit at all.

Be deliberate in instilling the value of church multiplication in the thinking of your church planters. Unless church multiplication is a major part of their original vision statement, it may get lost in the pressures of planting their own church. Early in the process, ask planters to spell out exactly what support for church multiplication means—they'll need to be specific in terms of personnel, prayer, finances, and other resources. You and your team will no doubt find it easy to put forth a number of scriptures to support the case for the financial support of church multiplication. The ministry of the Apostle Paul as described in Acts and his epistles will supply many examples as well as an occasional admonition.

One of the challenges in working with new churches is finding creative ways to give.

One recently planted church set up a partnership with their denomination. The denomination funds plants at a rate of $2000 per month, but does not fund planters—they are expected to be bivocational. The young parent church adopted a plant, matched that $2000 with an extra $2000 toward the planter's salary, and sent out an extra 45 people to go with the planter, along with their tithes and offerings. That strategy worked well for the plant, and the young parent church doubled in a year.

God sometimes calls us to dramatic steps of faith in giving to church multiplication. Yet we sometimes forget that a danger also exists on the opposite end of the spectrum: overfunding a new church can encourage dependency and can actually be damaging to a blossoming movement.

A Honduran pastor once warned an American church multiplication leader working in Honduras about helping too much with building programs or workers' expenses: "A demon rides in on every dollar which come from the United States." That multiplication leader, George Patterson, explained the admonition: "Probably nothing stifles the reproduction of churches in another culture more than outside funding. It carries a subtle form of control; a person who receives it feels morally obligated to do what the outsiders say, since they control the flow of the funds. Subsidizing new churches from the outside in any culture can stifle giving by the local people.... Satan whispers to them, 'Why plant more churches? You do not receive enough help now as it is.'"

Money is often one of the most common objections to church planting among potential parent churches. Yet in many cases, church multiplication need not be prohibitively expensive. Patterson recommends, "For church reproduction among the very poor people, use non-funded, low budget, or no budget programs —nothing beyond what local participants can provide. Let pastors start out being bivocational. Let new, poor churches have several unpaid elders (co-pastors) who share the pastoral responsibilities. We came to see very plainly that even the poorest of churches, if they give sacrificially or tithe, soon met their basic needs and their members escaped from their painful poverty.... It was now obvious; we rob the poor of a blessing if we do not encourage them to give what they can."

Reference: Patterson, George & Scoggins, Richard. *Church Multiplication Guide: Helping Churches to Reproduce Locally and Abroad* (Pasadena, CA: William Carey Library, 1993), pp. 44-45

Increasing financial resources

As you think about funding church multiplication movements, plan beyond the immediate future. The need for funding will only increase as a movement takes off. Currently available funds will not be sufficient to carry plans forward, develop a strategy for increasing financial support as the movement grows. Regularly review projected support that will become available as you multiply new, giving churches.

Spend some time with your team in "prayerful dreaming" and see what develops. What are some other possibilities for funding that did not come to mind at the beginning of the process? How can they be developed and the funds released? Once a movement has begun, unexpected sources of money can appear.

An inner city church plant served a population in which 70% of regular attendees were under age 18. Due to the community service nature of that ministry, the new church was able to attract a builder who was willing to construct a building at no cost.

A similar urban church plant was highly involved in serving the surrounding community in practical ways. It eventually attracted the attention of the county government, which voted to sell the church land at cost. The county council meeting was like a testimonial meeting, with person after person sharing how this church was transforming the community for the better.

A church planter was approached by two men he didn't know who had been watching his ministry and they donated one and a half million dollars.

Once the fruitfulness of a ministry becomes apparent in the community, unexpected opportunities often present themselves. Faithfulness demonstrated seems to attract the necessary resources at the right time. Pastor after pastor and planter after planter has found that when they stepped out on faith and needed the money, it was there.

Short checklist

Use the following checklist to evaluate the overall health and functionality of your church multiplication funding system. You may find it wise to describe certain areas in addition to checking them off. Any areas that you cannot check off should be incorporated into your future planning exercises. The Quick Find numbers of potentially helpful CompuCoach On-line documents have also been included. If you have not already printed these out, you may wish to do so before you work through this checklist with your team.

DEVELOPING FINANCIAL SUPPORT

- *QuickFind:* GD5231 *Finances for church planting*
- All currently available funds for church planting in our district have been identified.
- Guidelines and procedures for distributing these funds in an effective and equitable manner have been developed.
- Plans to tap other likely sources of support immediately "on the horizon" have been developed (communication pieces and processes have been created and key persons have been identified and contacted).
- A timeline for the development of other new, likely sources of funding has been created (with how much, who, what and when included).

TERMINATING INEFFECTIVE PROGRAMS AND REDIRECTING THE FUNDS

- *QuickFind:* WK937 *Ministry evaluation*
- WK940 *Making structures functional*
- CC1128 *What are the essentials for functional structures?*
- GD5865 *Guide 94: Making structures functional*
- A definition of ineffective programs has been developed and published.
- Methods for convincing others in our group that these programs are ineffective have been determined.
- Methods for convincing those involved in the ineffective programs that their programs are ineffective have been (prayerfully) developed.
- A procedure for terminating and redirecting funds from ineffective programs is in place.
- A system for ensuring follow-through in the termination of ineffective programs and the redirecting of funds is in place.

Afterword

After having read this book, consider.... What will your legacy be? What will your church's legacy be? What is your role in God's plan for the coming of his kingdom? God calls us to be ever-mindful of the future... remembering the beauty of the prophecy of Revelation 7:9-17:

> [9]*After this I looked and there before me was a great multitude that no one could count, from every nation, tribe, people and language, standing before the throne and in front of the Lamb. They were wearing white robes and were holding palm branches in their hands.* [10]*And they cried out in a loud voice: "Salvation belongs to our God, who sits on the throne, and to the Lamb."* [11]*All the angels were standing around the throne and around the elders and the four living creatures. They fell down on their faces before the throne and worshiped God,* [12]*saying: "Amen! Praise and glory and wisdom and thanks and honor and power and strength be to our God for ever and ever. Amen!"* [13]*Then one of the elders asked me, "These in white robes—who are they, and where did they come from?"* [14]*I answered, "Sir, you know."* [15]*And he said, "These are they who have come out of the great tribulation; they have washed their robes and made them white in the blood of the Lamb. Therefore, "they are before the throne of God and serve him day and night in his temple; and he who sits on the throne will spread his tent over them.* [16]*Never again will they hunger; never again will they thirst. The sun will not beat upon them, nor any scorching heat.* [17]*For the Lamb at the center of the throne will be their shepherd; he will lead them to springs of living water. And God will wipe away every tear from their eyes."*

That is where we are headed... that is the plan God has for his church: people from every tribe and nation gathered around the throne worshipping him. No more hunger, no more thirst—God wiping every tear from our eyes. What a beautiful vision of the future. Yet what's to happen between now and then? How do we get from here to there? For every nation, tribe and tongue to be reached, we need more churches that are reaching the harvest. We need churches starting churches starting churches.... multiplication movements that raise up leaders from the harvest and send them back out into the harvest. That's how the harvest will be transformed into the kingdom. One day we will all gather around the throne of God worshipping him in his glory throughout all eternity.

It's time to take a step of faith. We can all do something, so at least take whatever the next step is for you. Please contact us if there is any way we can serve you as you work toward the glory of the future kingdom.

For this reason I kneel before the Father, [15]from whom his whole family[1] in heaven and on earth derives its name. [16]I pray that out of his glorious riches he may strengthen you with power through his Spirit in your inner being, [17]so that Christ may dwell in your hearts through faith. And I pray that you, being rooted and established in love, [18]may have power, together with all the saints, to grasp how wide and long and high and deep is the love of Christ, [19]and to know this love that surpasses knowledge—that you may be filled to the measure of all the fullness of God. [20]Now to him who is able to do immeasurably more than all we ask or imagine, according to his power that is at work within us, [21]to him be glory in the church and in Christ Jesus throughout all generations, forever and ever! Amen.

Bibliography

(works directly referenced)

www.coachnet.org

Starting Church-starting Churches by Carol Davis, Copyright 1990, Carol Davis, Global Spectrum: The Urban Group

The Celtic Way of Evangelism: How Christianity Can Reach the West... Again by George G. Hunter III

Out of Ashes by Keith Phillips

Prayer Shield, C. Peter Wagner

A Fresh Perspective of Paul's Missionary Strategies: The Mentoring for Multiplication Model Neil Cole, 1998

Raising Leaders for the Harvest by Robert E. Logan and Neil Cole (St. Charles, IL, ChurchSmart Resources, 1996)

Planting New Churches in a Postmodern Age by Ed Stetzer

Ministering Cross-Culturally: An Incarnational Model for Personal Relationships Lingenfelter, Sherwood and Mayers, Marvin.

Empowering Leaders Through Coaching, Steve Ogne and Tom Nebel (St. Charles, IL, ChurchSmart Resources, 1996)

Church Multiplication Guide: Helping Churches to Reproduce Locally and Abroad, George Patterson & Richard Scoggins

That None Should Perish, Ed Silvoso

Home Groups for Urban Cultures, Mike Neuman, (Pasadena, CA: William Carey Library, 1999) p. 7.

Leading and Managing your Church by Robert E. Logan and Carl George (Grand Rapids, MI Baker/Revell, 1994)

Training for Selection Interviewing, Dr. Charles Ridley (St. Charles, IL ChurchSmart Resources, 1997)

The Institute for Natural Church Development International at www.ncd-international.org.

Historical Development of the Christian Movement, Dr. Paul Pierson, course offered by Fuller Theological Seminary

Honduran church growing through house fellowships by Nathan Hege, (Pulse, January 8, 1993)

The Church Planter's Toolkit, by Robert E. Logan and Steve Ogne (St. Charles, IL, ChurchSmart Resources, 1996)

Coaching 101 and *Coaching 101 Handbook* by Robert E. Logan and Sherilyn Carlton (St. Charles, IL, ChurchSmart Resources, 2003)

Disciples Are Made, Not Born, Walter Henrichsen p. 142

Why reinvent the wheel

CoachNet's online resources and planter community have the quick answers you're looking for while starting and multiplying churches. Network and get the insights you need to accomplish the goals God has set before you.

Interact with other church planters and work together to solve new problems being faced.

It's time.
CONNECT WITH US.

Beyond Church Planting

Robert E. Logan & Neil Cole

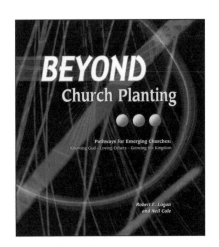

Authentic kingdom ministry flows out of who God is ... who we are ... how we relate to each other ... and how we fulfill God's purpose for his people. If you want to plant a church that ...

- Experiences God
- Cultivates true followers of Jesus Christ
- Develops organically within the culture
- Empowers its members to serve fruitfully
- Grows and reproduces itself

Then Beyond Church Planting is for you!

Forged out of the crucible of experience, this groundbreaking resource will help you avoid the mistakes of the past and gain insights that will pave the way for the emergence of fruitful multiplication of disciples, leaders, churches, and movements.

The combined church planting experience of the authors: **Robert Logan & Neil Cole** and contributing authors: **Mike Perkinson & Tom Johnston** - spans more than seven decades and has catalyzed the planting of thousands of new churches worldwide.

This resource kit includes a three-ring binder notebook, audio CD's and the author's powerpoint presentation on CD.

Price $95.00

1-800-253-4276

The Church Planter's Toolkit

Robert E. Logan

The premier resource for church planters! Combining the wisdom and expertise of Bob Logan and Steve Ogne, The Church Planter's Toolkit offers clear objectives that all church planters need to consider.

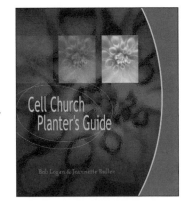

The Church Planter's Toolkit includes 12 audio CD's as well as detailed checklists and action planning worksheets to form a comprehensive package for church planters and their supervisors.

Beginning with spiritual foundations, you will learn how to develop effective strategies for starting healthy churches that are applicable in any context.

Logan and Ogne use an easy to understand life-cycle model to describe the phase of new church development (conception, prenatal, birth, growth and reproduction). All the key issues within one phase must be addressed before moving on to the next phase of development, otherwise, significant problems can arise in the new church.

Price $95.00

Cell Church Planter's Guide

Robert E. Logan & Jeannette Buller

The Cell Church Planter's Guide provides practical, step-by-step instructions to guide you as you establish a vision, gather a team, start your first cell groups, and launch your first celebration. Through a seven-stage church planting process, Logan and Buller will help you shape your journey to become a thriving cell church. As your church moves through these stages, you will find yourself returning to the hands-on tools provided to help you as you grow. This kit comes with ten cassette tapes and a notebook.

Price $95.00

Big Dreams in Small Places

Tom Nebel

For millions of Americans, small towns are places to live, work, make friends, raise their families, and die. It's a place of tradition, relatives and friends. Most small communities are typically secure, progressive, wonderful, authentic, vibrant, healthy… and needy. They represent a huge mission field that is ripe for a relevant gospel witness.

This book is written to inspire, encourage and challenge anyone who has ever thought of planting a new church to consider the possibility of living that adventure in the context of a small town. May your heart begin to beat a little faster for such an adventure as you read these pages.

Price $12.00

Church Planting Landmines

Tom Nebel & Gary Rohrmayer

We don't like to talk about failure. Church planters who fail do not speak at our conferences or write books. We hold up the successes and then wonder why so many church planters are surprised by hardships and overwhelmed by failure.

Learning from failure is a key concept in life and successful church planting. When asked about his hundreds of failed attempts to invent the lightbulb before experiencing success, Thomas Edison simply said that he had discovered all the ways not to produce the lightbulb. Church planting is no different. It needs to be seen as a process of "failing forward."

Church Planting Landmines looks at many of the issues that can bring failure and gives practical advice on how to avoid these mistakes.

Listen and learn from those who have stepped on some of these landmines. Keep failing forward!

Price $12.00